We are particularly grateful to Marley Floors, who supplied the flooring for the exhibition, as well as a number of individuals who have generously supported the exhibition: Mr and Mrs Federico Ceretti, Guy and Marion Naggar, and The Speyer Family Foundation, Inc. We would also like to express our gratitude to Richard and Judith Greer, Louise Blouin MacBain as well as Mark Hix for generously supporting the opening celebrations. As always, we are indebted to the Council of the Serpentine Gallery for their ongoing commitment.

We would also like to thank the Daiwa Anglo Japanese Foundation, Japan 21 and the Japan Foundation for contributing to the Education Programme accompanying the Tomoko Takahashi exhibition.

I extend my thanks to Rochelle Steiner, Chief Curator of the Serpentine Gallery and curator of this exhibition, who has contributed an insightful text to this publication. We are also grateful to Lorrie Mack for her editorial expertise. The publication has been designed by Frith Kerr and Amelia Noble of Kerr/Noble, with installation photography by Stephen White, who showed ingenuity in producing a catalogue that includes images of this new commission. We are also grateful to Bob Pain and Lorraine Sandy at Omnicolour for producing the artist's handsome Limited Edition Print.

Not least, my thanks go to all the members of the Serpentine Gallery team for their enthusiasm and commitment to this project and, in particular, Mike Gaughan, Gallery Manager, and Kathryn Rattee, Exhibition Organizer, who worked closely with the artist throughout the development of the project. Sally Tallant, Head of Education and Public Programmes, and her team organized the series of projects and activities that accompany the exhibition.

Julia Peyton-Jones
Director

Tomoko Takahashi
Deep Sea Diving/Dive 3: H.Q. 2002
Installation at Kunsthalle Bern, Switzerland
Courtesy of the artist and Hales Gallery
© 2005 Tomoko Takahashi; Photo: Tomoko Takahashi

The Order of Things [1]

'The world is full of objects, more or less interesting;
I do not wish to add any more.' Douglas Huebler [2]

Tomoko Takahashi's new commission, *my play-station at serpentine 2005*, comprises over 7,600 objects, mostly used or second hand, that she has been amassing for more than six months. Among them are a chemistry set, a miniature Christmas tree, an empty tool box, more than a dozen sewing machines (antique and modern, functioning and broken), a turquoise xylophone, a hula hoop covered in gold tape, two rolls of Astroturf, 20 orange school chairs, and a pair of yellow gloves. Takahashi learned that the Henry Cole Wing of the Victoria and Albert Museum was being renovated, and scavenged the remains. The Royal Parks contributed old fencing, a rusty boat, crowd-control barriers and a machine for spreading fertilizer, among other miscellaneous materials. Scaffolding, vitrines, an old staircase, cables and transformers were brought up from the Serpentine's basement. News of a fellow artist moving to another city prompted her to empty his studio of desks, shelves and a scanner. She happened on a full skip en route to a car-boot sale and helped herself to its contents. With the assistance of the Serpentine's staff, her friends, and a group of willing collaborators – including two east-end schools, a toy library, a recycling centre, and several like-minded 'collectors' – arrangements were made for items to be set aside, transported and added to the installation. Takahashi happily takes the opportunity to collect what others leave behind.

Based on her densely filled, room-sized works of art, it would be fair to call Takahashi a collector of the most obsessive degree. Like her work, her studio and living spaces are crammed with orderly stacks and random piles of *things*. Judging by the thousands of diverse objects that fill the Serpentine's galleries alone, it would seem as if she hoards everything she encounters and incorporates it into her art. On closer inspection, however, it becomes apparent that Takahashi does not collect indiscriminately: she is highly discerning in her hunt for materials. Among the clutter of a jumble sale, basement, skip or junk heap, she searches for precisely the right items and rejects those that are not to her liking. (For the most part, she prefers used goods without logos or specific brand associations.) Her passion to accumulate objects is balanced by a careful selection process during which she sifts and sorts the treasures she has gathered, applying a singular logic and form of connoisseurship whose rules are known only to her.

From the time she began thinking about her commission for the Serpentine, Takahashi was clear that she was looking for games and toys, but not dolls. Multiple copies of the same game were welcomed and there are, for example, three sets of *Monopoly* and two sets of *Yahtzee* included in the piece. Throughout the gathering process she was also interested in office-related objects such as typewriters and computers ('the older the better – they don't have to function') and telephones ('can they be wired to ring in the gallery?'), but not conventional studio materials or art supplies. Domestic appliances such as sewing and washing machines were on her 'shopping list'. She focused on items that make noise or move – remote control toys were deemed 'excellent' – and she adds kinetic energy to the piece with sensors and timers. Rounding out the installation are a number of elements that, over the course of her career, have become part of her standard vocabulary – among them, gaffer tape, clocks, desk lamps, road signs and playing cards.

Although it is easy to describe the objects Takahashi works with as 'rubbish' (a designation the artist herself rejects[3]), her installations contain no household waste in the usual sense of food scraps, newspapers, everyday packaging and the like. Rather, they comprise unwanted, mundane and, at times, obsolete domestic and office objects that have been found, donated or purchased inexpensively. After all, which is the better way to dispose of an old refrigerator, typewriter, mobile phone or computer that has been upgraded to a later model? Throw it away, or attempt to find it a new home and give it a second life? By bringing such items into her installations, Takahashi not only imbues them with new purpose, she also highlights the prevailing Western worship of the new, in the service of which fully functioning items are regularly cast aside.

Takahashi began working with found objects around 1994, as a student at London's Goldsmiths College. Although she was trained as a painter at Tama Art University in Tokyo and originally made surrealistic landscape paintings, her experiences at art school in London provided new-found freedom in terms of working across media. She has commented, 'I want to liberate things from imposed rules',[4] and she achieves this by altering the purpose as well as the context of the objects she brings into her work. Takahashi turned to the materials at hand to create her award-winning installation at the1997 *EAST International*, a group exhibition at the Norwich Gallery, which first brought critical attention to her work. In this two-part installation, *The Painting Storage Department* and *Left Overs from the Painting Department*, she utilized items that had been cleared to make room for the exhibition, bringing them back into the gallery, assembling them into an installation, and creating what has become her signature, low-tech aesthetic. Critics have often commented on the artist's perceived interest in recycling, but her decision to work with used and obsolete objects is rooted less in ecological or environmental consciousness than in practicality – she uses what's available. Similarly, with its abundance of consumer products, Takahashi's work can be interpreted as a commentary on capitalism and general excess, but her approach is more responsive to particular sites and personal situations than it is intent on social or political commentary.[5]

Takahashi typically incorporates references to the site in which she works and the specific conditions of her life into her installations. For example, for her 1998 work at the Drawing Center in New York (a space that features exhibitions of drawings and works on paper), she brought two suitcases full of personal papers from London, including letters, proposals and junk mail, which she displayed on the gallery walls in an abstract arrangement, but only after having crossed out and obliterated all of the text and writing with pen. In the same year, her installation *Clockwork at Hales* in London was filled with a seemingly endless array of broken and functioning clocks, a reference to the then-tentative nature of her visa status in the UK and her receipt of 'notification to leave the country within 28 days'. According to the artist, 'I was thinking of "TIME" all the time in those days. I and my friends collected more than 300 clocks from neumerous (sic) car-boot sales for this show. All the clocks were intentionally somehow "broken", but, they were still ticking away.'[6]

Similarly *my play-station at serpentine 2005* reflects the artist's own interests and focuses generally on a series of themes, including play and rules (through the use of toys and games), learning (using teaching tools, objects from schools and museums), work (incorporating office-related items such as desks and lamps), and the outdoors (with

Tomoko Takahashi
Clockwork at Hales 1998
Installation at Hales Gallery, London
Courtesy of the artist and Hales Gallery
© 2005 Tomoko Takahashi; Photo: Tomoko Takahashi

Tomoko Takahashi
The Painting Department Storage 1997
Installation for EAST at Norwich Gallery
Courtesy of the artist and Hales Gallery
© 2005 Tomoko Takahashi

Tomoko Takahashi
The Drawing Room 1998
Installation at The Drawing Center, New York
Tate, Presented by the Patrons of New Art
(Special Purchase Fund) 2002
Photo courtesy of the artist and Hales Gallery
© 2005 Tomoko Takahashi

materials from the Park). The experience of *my play-station at serpentine 2005* begins outside the Gallery: a collage made of box tops and packaging from dozens of toys – in particular, construction toys – appears on the building's east windows. Like a shop display visible only from the outside, these elements set the tone for what lies within. Throughout the Serpentine is a vast array of toys and games ranging from common board games (*Monopoly, The Game of Life* and *mah-jong*) to obscure ones (*Mid-Life Crisis, Dizzy Dinosaur* and *Fleas on Fred*) as well as the pieces of over one hundred jigsaw puzzles and thousands of playing cards. Takahashi's interest in games, which have appeared in a number of her previous projects and form an overarching theme in her work, is rooted in her fascination with their inherent rules and the order they impose on play. She uses such rules to govern her own creative process: for example, the Serpentine s health and safety stipulation that she leave a path measuring 120 cm wide for public access through the space resulted in her marking this dimension repeatedly on the floor of each room and doorway with a white dotted line. While some artists might view this 'rule' as a limitation, Takahashi turns it into a creative tool.

Games not only feature as objects within Takahashi's installations, they have also inspired related activities including a public game of Tag (which the she calls 'It'), organized by her and artist Simon Faithfull at Clissold Park in London in 2000 and again on the lawn outside the Serpentine in conjunction with this exhibition. In their version, the game is played at dusk under ultraviolet light and projected onto a large screen. The players wear white hats so they appear on the screen as dots that form seemingly random patterns as they move. Since the rules of the game are well defined, what appears to be chaos actually follows a prescribed plan.

Takahashi's interest in games also extends to what might be considered her personal obsession: the card game of Patience, known in North America as Solitaire. Having grown up in a family that often played cards, she started to play Patience on a trip from London to Edinburgh. She became addicted to the game and has described 'playing Patience as a way of tidying up, sorting things out, and helping to find a new route'. According to Takahashi, 'it's working with and having a fight with oneself, a bit like what happens when making a work'.[7] Patience can be seen as a metaphor for the artist's obsessive working process: she works alone with her chosen materials to organize them into highly ordered sequences. Her love of this card game extends to collaborating with artist Ella Gibbs to orchestrate 24- and 48-hour events called *The Day of Patience* and *Area of Patience* respectively, both in 1999, that invited the public to learn and to play various forms of the traditional card game. These events were followed by *The Room of Patience* at Tate Britain, staged again with Gibbs, in conjunction with Takahashi's Turner Prize nomination in 2000. In addition, they have published three versions of *The Booklet of Patience* (1999 and 2000), which outline the history of the game as well as rules, strategies and tips for players.

Inside the Serpentine, Takahashi utilizes the boundaries of the Serpentine's individual gallery spaces to organize her chosen themes into a series of distinct, multi-sensory environments, each with a different character. She refers to the first exhibition space, the south gallery, as the 'Reception'. It is dominated by the inventory of the contents of the exhibition, a list that was created by the Serpentine's installation team at the artist's request as all of the objects were moved into the Gallery over a five-day period. The list, which also appears within this catalogue, is not categorized in any systematic way; instead it documents the order in which the more than 7,600 objects arrived and the sheer abundance of Takahashi's collecting habits. In the east gallery, Takahashi has created an 'Office' with desks, chairs and ringing telephones. Unlike a functioning work space, though, the gallery is darkened and includes a toy racetrack with electric cars set in motion. She refers to the west gallery as the 'Garden', which overlooks Kensington Gardens and includes outdoor materials scavenged from the Royal Parks.

The Serpentine's large, central north gallery contains an exuberant display that the artist refers to as the 'Kitchen/Headquarters'. It includes washing machines, a toy microwave painted red, an oven, a sink, assorted cutlery and kitchen utensils, kettles, tables and chairs interspersed within an array of game boards, game pieces, puzzle pieces and cards. Hung around the room at varying heights is a collection of glass windows in wooden frames, which may have come from museum display cases and evoke the feeling of an old-fashioned picture gallery. Each framed window is presented with an accompanying number, recalling museum labelling systems; instead of being indexed to a list of identifying captions, the numbers indicate the order in which the

Tomoko Takahashi and Ella Gibbs
Day of Patience 1999
24-hour project at belt a space in between, London
Courtesy of the artist and Hales Gallery
© 2005 Tomoko Takahashi and Ella Gibbs

windows were installed. Juxtaposed with these frames are hundreds of playing cards stapled to the walls in a structured format that follows the artist's prescribed rules for 'North Gallery Patience', as she calls it, which appear in her handwriting in the doorway just outside the space. There she also notes what she considers to be 'cheating'. The logic of this 'game' is almost a conceptual procedure that she carries out as a matter of course – playing by the rules she set up until the walls have been filled and her desired sequences of cards have been completed.

Takahashi's installations have frequently been described as organized or disciplined chaos: they are at once casual scatterings and systematic arrangements. Because they feature objects side by side that are both related and unrelated, old and new, found and borrowed, useful and useless, mundane and rare, at first glance, her works resemble haphazard heaps. They are, more accurately, complex three-dimensional collages with an internal logic that the artist uses to structure and order objects within space. Characteristic of her work, many of her objects at the Serpentine have been selected for their intended functions: equipment like scaffolding, tables and vitrines provides physical support for stacking and displaying other items and achieving verticality in the overall composition. Meanwhile, the typical, specified use of other objects has been redefined. For example, the standard desk lamps in this installation create ambient lighting within the Gallery rather than perform their original function – to illuminate small work spaces. Likewise, washing machines produce sound, making repetitive noises as they go through their various cycles. It is significant that she does not merely stack objects on top of each other but lays them out making an idiosyncratic archaeology of the things that surround her. A sense of rhythm is created through the repetition of elements, forms and colours, and the installation is punctuated by sound and kinetic elements that are rigged up with sensors and timers to be triggered by the movement of people in the space.

The artist's interest in the sound generated by the various elements has inspired a collaboration with The Leafcutter John Orchestra, which has been developed as a unique event held within the Serpentine exhibition. In this sound performance, musicians will transform Takahashi's work itself into an instrument and create a score, adding to the various background noises created by the objects. In the spirit of a performance by experimental musician John Cage, the result is a spontaneous piece of music that is dependent upon chance occurrences involving both people and objects in the space.

Takahashi's installations are awesome displays of stuff. Visitors cannot help but feel amazed, and at times overwhelmed, not only by the sheer volume of items but also by her ability to create a universe from otherwise random objects. Her method of collecting, classifying and displaying heterogeneous items is not unlike that of 16th and 17th century collectors who travelled the world, amassed rare, unique, and unfamiliar objects, and proudly displayed them for both public and private viewing in *Wunderkammern*: cabinets of curiosities. *Wunderkammern* were typically filled from top to bottom with a stunning array of natural and man-made objects past and present intended to provoke surprise and wonder. These collections from both near and far not only reflected the interest in the intellectual and geographical exploration of the day, they also mark the origins of modern museums, which were born out of encyclopaedic collecting patterns.[8] Takahashi's installations are very much like modern-day wonder cabinets, displaying multitudes of diverse souvenirs from a range of sources[9]; but rather than focusing on the rare and exotic, she is fascinated by mundane, readymade objects.

The history of Readymades in contemporary art and the roots of installation as an artistic format are both closely linked with the work of pivotal artists Kurt Schwitters and Marcel Duchamp at the beginning of the 20th century. Schwitters's three-dimensional collage environment, *Merzbau*, 1923-37, combined painting, assemblage, sculpture and architecture, as well as integrated non-artistic materials that had previously been used in collage. Schwitters approached art making through playful experimentation, and unabashedly considered all found objects and forms of daily refuse as viable artistic materials. By bringing these together intuitively rather than following a pre-determined theory or plan, the artist liberated himself 'from the conventional rules and aims of art'.[10] As *Merzbau* grew, the full-scale, all-enveloping environment came to include dramatic lighting; at times, it was even animated by live guinea pigs. Eventually the construction overtook the artist's studio, encompassing three rooms in the Schwitters home in Hanover before it was destroyed during an air raid in 1943. Importantly, the artist conceived *Merzbau* as a '*work in process*' that was perpetually

Kurt Schwitters
Merzbau c1932 (destroyed 1943)
Installation view from side stairway entrance
Courtesy of Kurt Schwitters Archive, Sprengel Museum
Hannover © VG Bild-Kunst, Bonn © DACS 2005
Photo: Wilhelm Redemann

unfinished 'as a matter of principle'.[11] It expanded so extensively that the original architecture of the building began to disappear: for Schwitters it was not just 'a matter of painting or using walls, but of completely dismantling the old function of the space and turning his studio into a wholly unconstrained space for experiencing art'.[12]

While Schwitters built *Merzbau* in an isolated place over the course of many years, Duchamp, who forever changed the course of art by transforming a urinal into a sculpture entitled *Fountain*, 1917, infiltrated two seminal avant-garde exhibitions with purposefully temporary gestures. At the *International Exposition of Surrealism* in Paris in 1938, he created *1,200 Bags of Coal* by suspending bags from the ceiling and placing a 'stove' – a makeshift brazier created with an old barrel fitted with a light bulb – in the centre of the floor.[13] In doing so he transformed the exhibition space, inverting it through the implication that the seemingly heavy items were placed on the ceiling and the source of light was on the ground. Four years later, at the *First Papers of Surrealism* in New York, Duchamp's *Mile of String*, 1942, was a meandering, web-like maze strung from floor to ceiling and wall to wall among the other works in the exhibition. Here he connected all aspects of the room: the other art works on display, the exhibition space and the viewers were all ensnared within the piece, essentially co-opting the contents of the exhibition and the gallery space. His transformations of exhibition spaces and the resulting disruption of the way viewers experienced art were crucial to the development of installation that followed by artists working throughout the 20th century.

In his series of important essays 'Inside the White Cube', first published in *Artforum* in 1976 [14], critic Brian O'Doherty (aka artist Patrick Ireland) was among the earliest to outline the conditions that would come to define installation. Citing Schwitters' *Merzbau* as 'the first example of a "gallery" as a chamber of transformation' [15] and Duchamp's *1,200 Bags of Coal* as 'the first time an artist subsumed an entire gallery in a single gesture', [16] O'Doherty focused on the then-radical ways in which these artists forced a reconsideration of the relationship between a work of art and its context. Eluding formal definition, installation has developed extensively since the 1960s to include a wide variety of artistic practices. Ranging from the alteration of one's experience of a space using traditional, non-traditional and/or mixed media, to the activity (performed either by artists or curators) of arranging and exhibiting found elements or art objects within a site, these different forms of installation are united by the roles viewers play in them: they must enter, both physically and mentally, into the space and allow themselves to be enveloped in a setting that has been created to evoke a particular response. Viewers are transformed from passive spectators into active participants, and the divisions between subject and object, viewer and viewed are broken down.

Artists may, for example, transform physical space and challenge perceptions of the surrounding environment, as exemplified by Olafur Eliasson's *The Weather Project*, 2004, at Tate Modern, which has strong historical links to the American Light and Space artists of the 1960s and 1970s. Or they can create elaborate theatrical tableaux in which visitors experience narratives laid out in three-dimensional space, as in the installations by Russian-born Ilya and Emilia Kabakov, German Gregor

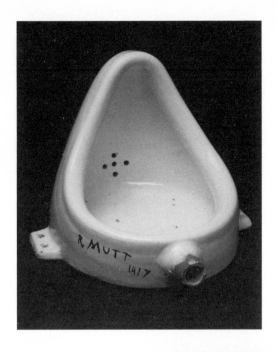

Marcel Duchamp
Fountain 1950 (replica of 1917 original)
Readymade (glazed sanitary china with black paint)
Philadelphia Museum of Art: Gift (by exchange) of
Mrs Herbert Cameron Morris, 1998
© Succession Marcel Duchamp/ADAGP, Paris and
DACS, London 2005; Photo: Graydon Wood

Marcel Duchamp
Mile of String 1942
Installation in First Papers of Surrealism, New York
Philadelphia Museum of Art: Gift of Jacqueline,
Paul and Peter Matisse in memory of their mother
Alexina Duchamp
© Succession Marcel Duchamp/ADAGP, Paris and
DACS, London 2005; Photo: John D Schiff

Peter Fischli and David Weiss
Empty Room 1995-96
Polyurethane, paint
Collection Walker Art Center, Minneapolis
T.B. Walker Acquisition Fund, 1996
© 2005 Peter Fischli and David Weiss

Schneider or UK-based Mike Nelson. In some cases, such as Schneider's project in London commissioned by Artangel, *Die Familie Schneider*, 2004, in which the public was invited into two identical apartments in east London, visitors are made to feel like voyeurs when they enter and encounter a woman in the kitchen washing dishes or a naked man in the shower. Most relevant for contextualizing Takahashi's work, however, are contemporary installations based on the accumulation and display of everyday objects, such as the meticulously handcrafted arrangements of seemingly readymade paper cups, boards and paint buckets by the Swiss duo Peter Fischli and David Weiss that simulate debris found behind the scenes of a museum – in store rooms, for instance, or during the preparation of an exhibition. Also providing comparisons are Jason Rhoades' provocative arrangements of carefully ordered new objects that form webs of associations; Sarah Sze's elaborate assemblages in which an abundance of real objects from daily life such

Jason Rhoades
My Brother/Brancusi 1995
Installation view
Carpet, wood, steel, donut machine,
donut mix, small gasoline engines,
various tools, plastic, drill and whisk
Courtesy of David Zwirner, New York
© 2005 Jason Rhoades

as toothpicks, pens, paperclips, plants, and sweets are transformed into whimsical, albeit highly structured, creations; and Mark Dion's presentation of objects based on scientific, archaeological or historical classifications.

Takahashi's work can also be viewed historically, in light of artists working in the 1960s who not only incorporated everyday objects into their work, but also created installations and events beyond the traditional parameters of museums and galleries and, in doing so, opened up the range of forms art would take. In 1960, Fluxus artist Ben Vautier created *Le Magasin* (*The Shop*), a 'gallery' where he displayed and sold an array of everyday items. Conceived as a 'living sculpture', the artist himself was on view in the shop window, surrounded by objects of daily life such as a bed, table, chairs, television, and cooking utensils.[17] Shortly after, from December 1960 to January 1961, Pop artist

Claes Oldenburg opened *The Store* in New York, a 'gallery-studio-performance-environment' that resembled a commercial shop and sold a variety of hand-crafted 'consumer goods,' including hamburgers, pies, shoes, clothing, and jewellery, all of which were created out of plaster and painted by the artist.[18]

Further links can be drawn between Takahashi's work and Happenings — environmental performances initially presented in gallery spaces and later outdoors that were devoid of traditional narrative structure. They generally involved the spatial arrangement of objects or props and required the participation of both artist and viewers. Happenings were indebted to the action paintings of Jackson Pollock, which brought attention to the physical gestures and processes involved in making art, and to the experimental sound work of John Cage, which took spontaneity, improvisation and chance as its starting points. Originally called an 'action-collage', the first Happening in 1959 is credited to American Allan Kaprow, who utilized various materials such as foil, straw, canvas, photos and newspaper, and combined them as quickly as

possible within a gallery space or site.[19] In time he introduced flashing lights and other sensory elements such as buzzers, bells, and sounds from toys to engage viewers further in complete environments.

These works from the middle of the 20th century anticipated key qualities that would develop in installation work: the creation of environments; the display of objects in relation to one another and to the overall space; a performative quality on the part of the artist; and the incorporation of viewers as participants — all of which are present in Takahashi's work. And yet, while her installations share characteristics with those of artists both past and present, she puts her own, unique mark on them and the way they are created. **O**f critical importance to her is the a**b**ility t**o** occupy a site fully while she makes her work: to complete *my play-station at serpentine 2005*, she lived at the Gallery 24 hours a day for four weeks. In this sense, the experience of the installation is one of total immersion — not only for viewers, but for the artist as well. While the actual process of making her installations is not recorded in photographs or videos, the amount of time it takes to create each piece is documented by Takahashi as testimony to her stamina and the labour involved in her creative process, and as a way of marking time. On the first day of the installation, her handmade calendar came to fill an entire wall of the Serpentine's south gallery, recording her daily appointments, plans, ideas and deadlines. Likewise, in her self-designed *catalogue raisonné* that accompanied her exhibition at Kunsthalle Bern in 2002, she not only documents all of her work to date, but also identifies the number of days each piece took to create.

Additionally, a glimpse into her working process is implied through the handwritten notes, markings and other evidence generated over the course of the four weeks and incorporated into her final installation. At the Serpentine, her shopping lists, questions to ask the Gallery Manager, instructions to the technicians, measurements and *aide-memoires* sprung up daily, taped and written directly onto the walls. They remain and provide visitors with a glimpse into her personal habits; one message, left for the staff after a long night of work, says simply 'I'll be up around 1pm (13:00)'. Previous installations have included her cigarette **b**utts, duvet, alarm clock, and other personal items – all indicators of Takahashi's continual physical presence throughout the making of e**a**ch piece. These elements also serve as reminders that, for Takahashi, the gallery functions both as a working studio in which art is produced and as a stage for displaying the final product.

Takahashi's installations are temporary and ultimately ephemeral. While she does not invite visitors to interact with her installations during the course of the exhibition – the individual objects are not meant to be touched or rearranged by the publi**c** – she has stip**u**lated that the installation be dismantled on its final day in an event entitled *Serpentine take-away (loads of things must go!)*. In this way, Takahashi returns all the objects that comprise her installation to the everyday world from which they came – as durable goods rather than as art objects – and gives them yet another life. By investing objects, many of which are obsolete, with labour, they may have had value temporarily within the context of her installation. But, in the end, they revert to being ordinary, everyday things looking for a new purpo**s**e and a new home.

1. This title is inspired by Michel Foucault's *The Order of Things, An Archaeology of the Human Sciences* (New York: Random House, Inc, 1970)

2. Douglas Huebler, *January 5-31, 1969* (New York: Seth Siegelaub, 1969)

3. Rachel Withers, 'Tomoko Takahashi, Beaconsfield, London', *Frieze* (March-April 1998), p 84

4. Jemima Montagu, 'Tomoko Takahashi', *BBC-Arts*, accessed 7 November 2001 <http:www.bbc.co.uk/arts/news>

5. Rachel Taylor, 'Drawing Room', *Tate Online*, December 2003 <www.tate.org.uk>

6. *The Catalogue of Allmost All the Works Done By…Tomoko Takahashi (Between 1985-2002)*, (Bern: Kunsthalle Bern, 2002), p 20

7. Tomoko Takahashi and Ella Gibbs, *The Booklet of Patience* (London: Tablet, 1999), p 35. *The Booklet of Patience* was first produced in June 1999 (London: belt a space in between) and was reprinted in November 2000 (London: Tate) on the occasion of *The Room of Patience* at Tate Britain.

8. For discussions of *Wunderkammern*, see Oliver Impey and Arthur MacGregor, eds., *The Origins of Museums: The Cabinet of Curiosities in Sixteenth - and Seventeenth - Century Europe* (Oxford: Clarendon Press, 1985) and Joy Kenseth, 'A World of Wonders in One Closet Shut', *The Age of the Marvelous*, ed. Joy Kenseth (Hanover: Hood Museum of Art, Dartmouth College, 1991), p 25

9. A number of contemporary artists have created works that can be compared to *Wunderkammern*, many of which set out to examine the structures and underpinnings, both aesthetic and political, of museums and galleries. Among them, Claes Oldenburg created *Mouse Museum* (1965-77), a modern-day 'curiosity cabinet' in the shape of his signature, iconic mouse character and filled with found, altered and fabricated objects.

10. Isabel Schulz, '"What Would Life Be Without Merz?" On the Evolution and Meaning of Kurt Schwitters' Concept of Art', *Merz: In the Beginning was Merz, From Schwitters to the Present Day*, eds. Susanne Meyer-Büser and Karin Orchard (Ostfildern, Germany: Hatje Cantz, 2000), p 245

11. Susanne Meyer-Büser, 'On Disappearing in Space, Walk-in Collages from Schwitters to the Present Day', in *op cit.*, p 276

12. *Op cit.*, p 274

13. See Arturo Schwarz, *The Complete Works of Marcel Duchamp*, vol 2 (New York: Delano Greenidge Editions, 1997), pp 747-48. The bags in the installation were empty, but had previously been used to transport coal.

14. Brian O'Doherty's essays were originally printed in *Artforum* over a series of months in 1976 before being reprinted in *Inside the White Cube: The Ideology of the Gallery Space* (Santa Monica: Lapis Press, 1976, 1981, 1986 and 1999). Citations in this essay are from the original version in *Artforum*.

15. O'Doherty, 'Inside the White Cube, Part II, The Eye and The Spectator', *Artforum* (April 1976), p 30

16. O'Doherty, 'Inside the White Cube, Part III, Context as Content', *Artforum* (November 1976), p 40

17. See Paul Schimmel, *Out of Actions: between performance and the object, 1949-1979* (Los Angeles: The Museum of Contemporary Art and New York: Thames and Hudson, Ltd.,1988). See also Owen F Smith, 'Fluxus: A Brief History', In *The Spirit of Fluxus*, Elizabeth Armstrong and Joan Ruthfuss, eds. (Minneapolis: Walker Art Center, 1993)

18. Schimmel, *op cit.*, p 68. See also Schimmel, *Hand-Painted Pop: American Art in Transition 1955-62* (Los Angeles: The Museum of Contemporary Art and New York: Rizzoli International, 1992)

19. See Schimmel, *Out of Actions*, p 59. Originally cited in Adrian Henri, 'Allan Kaprow', *Total Art: Environments, Happenings, and Performance* (New York: Oxford University Press, 1974)

1 PLASTIC TOY KEYBOARD
1 TOY SLIDE
2 TOY SNOOKER & POOL SETS
1 ABACUS
1 YELLOW PLASTIC TOY SCHOOL BUS
1 FISHER-PRICE FARM TOY
1 PLASTIC RED-AND-WHITE TOY JEEP
1 PLASTIC FROG GAME
1 PLASTIC TOY ROCK GUITAR
2 HARRY POTTER LEGO SETS
1 PLASTIC TOY PINBALL MACHINE
1 PLASTIC TOY TOMY COMPUTER
1 VACUUM CLEANER ATTACHMENT
1 WHITE WIRE
1 BAG OF MULTICOLOURED FOAM JIGSAW PIECES
1 SOFT TOY RABBIT
1 BROKEN WOODEN BOARD GAME
2 SETS OF CHRISTMAS LIGHTS
1 YELLOW TIPPER TRUCK
1 MICROSCOPE
1 EL GRAN LINCE BOARD GAME
1 TOY CUTLERY SET
1 GREEN WOODEN TIPPER TRUCK
1 GOLF GAME
1 TOY CASSETTE PLAYER
1 RED ROYAL MAIL BAG
6 SMALL CLOWN FIGURINES
6 WOODEN PIECES FOR HOUSE-SHAPED JIGSAW
1 CHILD'S DESK
1 CHEMISTRY SET
1 POP UP PIRATE CHILDREN'S GAME
1 ZAXXON - FAMILY VERSION OF THE ARCADE GAME
1 BAG OF ASSORTED PLASTIC ANIMALS AND FIGURES
1 PLASTIC TOY WINGED HORSE
20 ASSORTED CHILDREN'S BOOKS
1 A SPY FOR A SPY MYSTERY JIGSAW PUZZLE
1 GIANT FARM FLOOR PUZZLE
1 FIRST KNITTING SET KIT
1 FAMOUS FIVE JIGSAW PUZZLE
1 FACE PAINTING KIT
1 BUILD-A-TOWN PUZZLE
1 TOTS TV FLOOR PUZZLE
1 DINOSAUR JIGSAW PUZZLE
1 FARM ANIMALS JIGSAW PUZZLE
1 SPIRAL STENCIL ART SET
1 EXPRESS TRAIN FLOOR PUZZLE
1 TALL STORIES GAME
1 ROBIN HOOD GAME
1 101 DALMATIANS PUZZLE
1 PUPPY IN MY POCKET GAME
1 PLASTIC TRAVEL CHESS SET
6 GIANT DICE
1 WALKIE-TALKIE POLICE STATION SET
1 MAISY'S GIANT SNAKES AND LADDERS BOARD GAME
3 COMPUTER MONITORS
3 COMPUTER KEYBOARDS
1 PC COMPUTER
1 MACINTOSH COMPUTER
1 SLIDE VIEWER WITH CARRIER CASE
1 PORTABLE TV
2 WHITE CABLES
1 NATIVITY STABLE
1 PLASTIC BOX OF CUTLERY
16 TENNIS BALLS
8 LONDON A-Z
15 ENCYCLOPAEDIA BRITANNICA BOOKS
2 BUNDLES OF WILDLIFE MAGAZINE
1 FAKE CHRISTMAS TREE
1 TOOL BOX
6 PARTS OF PLASTIC BABY ACTIVITY GAME
1 TURQUOISE TOY XYLOPHONE
1 PLAYSCHOOL PULL-ALONG DINOSAUR
1 PLASTIC TOY HOUSE WITH DOG AND CAT
1 PLASTIC TOY TORCH
1 DESK
1 METAL CABINET
1 CUPBOARD
10 LARGE GLASS DOORS WITH WOODEN FRAMES
1 PLASTIC OFFICE CHAIR
2 ROLLS ASTROTURF
1 METAL STEPLADDER
20 SMALL GLASS DOORS WITH WOODEN FRAMES
2 FILING CABINETS
1 FAKE CHRISTMAS TREE
2 METAL DESK TOPS
2 SETS OF WOODEN DESK LEGS
2 FAKE TREES
1 BLUE PORTABLE VACUUM CLEANER

1 PHILLIPS FACE TANNING MACHINE
2 OVAL GLASS AND WOODEN DOORS
1 HULA HOOP
2 BAGS OF MULTICOLOURED LEGO PIECES
1 BROKEN CAR SEAT IN TWO PARTS
1 ORANGE VACUUM CLEANER
1 WOODEN BOOKSHELF
1 WOODEN CUPBOARD
1 WOODEN TABLE WITH 4 CHAIRS
1 SMALL RADIATOR
1 WOODEN CHAIR WITH YELLOW CUSHION
1 CAR TYRE
18 GREY CHILDREN'S SCHOOL CHAIRS
20 ORANGE CHILDREN'S SCHOOL CHAIRS
6 BEIGE SCHOOL CHAIRS
1 SOFT TOY BELL
1 PLASTIC TOY SPACE SHUTTLE
1 PLASTIC TOY TEDDY
1 PLASTIC TOY CAROUSEL
1 PLASTIC MOUNTAIN WITH CAVE
1 PLASTIC TOY ACTIVITY SET
1 PLASTIC TOY WENDY HOUSE
1 PLASTIC TOY ELEPHANT
1 ORANGE PLASTIC TOY FIRE TRUCK
1 PLASTIC CHILD'S RATTLE
1 PLASTIC TOY SPEEDBOAT
1 BAG OF ASSORTED WOODEN JIGSAWS PIECES
1 PLASTIC TOY POLICE HEAD
1 PLASTIC TOY LUNCHBOX
1 PLASTIC TOY MAGGIE SIMPSON WIND-UP DOLL
1 DINOSAUR WIND-UP TOY
3 PLASTIC WATER PISTOLS
1 BOX OF ASSORTED PLASTIC CARS AND TOYS
2 PLASTIC TOY WALKIE-TALKIES
1 CHILD'S CAR SEAT
1 GREY OFFICE CHAIR
1 BROKEN WOODEN BATHROOM CABINET
1 LEATHER SHOPPING TROLLEY
1 PLASTIC TOY TANDEM BICYCLE
2 INFLATABLE PADDLING POOLS
1 PLASTIC NUMBERS COUNTING GAME
1 COFFEE URN
1 PLASTIC TOY SLIDE
1 TALK-TO-TEDDY TOY PHONE
2 BADMINTON RACKETS
1 PAIR OF GLOVES
1 PLASTIC TOY SEWING MACHINE WITH CASE
1 BLACK AND GREY PUSH CHAIR
1 EXERCISE BIKE
1 PLASTIC TOY TROLLEY
1 PLASTIC TOY BATH
1 BAG OF ASSORTED MULTICOLOURED WOODEN BLOCKS
1 BUCKET OF MULTICOLOURED DUPLO BRICKS
1 BUCKET OF MULTICOLOURED STICKLE BRICKS
1 KITCHEN SINK
1 WOODEN PUB STOOL
1 BROKEN WOODEN BROOM
1 WOODEN RESTAURANT SIGN
3 BICYCLE TYRES
2 BICYCLE WHEELS
1 RED AND BLACK FEATHER BOA
1 MEMO BOARD
1 WOODEN SIGN
2 WOODEN BOWLS
1 WASH BAG
1 SOFT TOY CAR
1 SOFT TOY DUCK
2 TOY PHONES
1 BAG OF FOAM JIGSAW PIECES
1 ELECTRONIC BUZZ LIGHTYEAR TOY FIGURE
1 PLASTIC TOY ACTIVITY HOUSE
1 THOMAS THE TANK ENGINE FELT GAME
1 NINJA TURTLES TOY FIGURE
1 102 DALMATIANS JIGSAW PUZZLE
1 TEDDY BEAR JIGSAW PUZZLE
1 WHO IS IN THE GARDEN? JIGSAW PUZZLE
4 BOB THE BUILDER JIGSAW PUZZLES
1 POWER RANGERS JIGSAW PUZZLE
1 BOX OF FUZZY FELT
1 PLASTIC CAR PUZZLE
1 BOX OF ASSORTED TOY FIGURES
1 METAL TELEVISION STAND
1 PLASTIC DISC
1 TIN OF ASSORTED PLASTIC TOYS
1 ACCESSING THE WEB BOOK
1 FENCING HELMET
1 GREY LAMPSHADE
1 GREY PLASTIC CASSETTE RECORDER
1 PLASTIC TOY WASHING MACHINE
1 BLACK LEATHER BRIEFCASE

5 WOODEN SHELVING BOXES
1 PLASTIC BUCKET
2 WOODEN BRUSHES
1 ELECTRIC CABLE
1 METAL RAZOR WIRE
1 PLASTIC JUG
1 BALL GAME
1 MANNEQUIN ARM
2 RUSTY METAL CONTAINERS
1 METAL MAGAZINE RACK
1 DOLL'S STRAW HAT
1 PAPER BAG OF ASSORTED TOYS
1 MECHANICAL TOY DIGGER TRUCK
2 GLASS LAMPSHADES
1 PLASTIC GLOBE
1 PLASTIC YELLOW CRANE
1 CAR RADIO
1 TOY BOXING BALL
2 SETS OF FAIRY LIGHTS WITH FRUIT-SHAPED BULBS
1 LAPTOP
1 ELECTRIC FAN
2 PEARL NECKLACES
2 TINSEL BALLS
1 SET OF FAIRY LIGHTS WITH STAR-SHAPED BULBS
4 MOTION DETECTORS
1 BROKEN FUSE BOX
1 PINK FEATHER BOA
1 BAG OF ASSORTED CHRISTMAS DECORATIONS
ASSORTED UNUSED ENVELOPES
ASSORTED UNUSED FILES
1 TELEPHONE HEAD SET
3 TUBES OF PAINT
1 METAL TEASPOON
1 BROKEN VACUUM CLEANER COVER
2 WHITE PLASTIC CONTAINERS
1 FOOTBALL
1 PLASTIC TOY TIPPER TRUCK
1 BAG OF ASSORTED PLASTIC TOYS
2 SETS OF BOULES
1 BLACK LEATHER SHOE
1 BLACK PLASTIC BIN
3 PLASTIC SERVING TRAYS
1 BAG OF PLASTIC SUCKERS
1 PLASTIC JIGSAW PUZZLE
1 PLASTIC PINK TOY TRUCK
1 WOODEN ALPHABET GAME
1 BAG OF ASSORTED PLASTIC TOYS
1 COLORAMA GAME
1 CHRISTMAS TREE STAND
1 BRITISH ISLES PICTURE PUZZLE
1 MONOPOLY BOARD GAME
3 GAME OF LIFE BOARD GAMES
2 SPEAKER PADS
1 MOUSE TRAP BOARD GAME
1 WOOD TOY GAME
1 SPEC BOARD GAME
4 FILING TRAYS
2 FIRE-FIGHTER FIGURES WITH REMOTE CONTROL
1 PLASTIC TOY OCTOPUS
1 PLASTIC TOY TRUCK
1 PLASTIC MECHANICAL RACING CAR
1 PLASTIC TOY CAR
1 WHEEL OF FORTUNE BOARD GAME
1 SPIDER MAN PLAYSET
1 CHILD'S PAPER TIMETABLE
2 BADMINTON RACKETS WITH COVERS
1 PLASTIC TOY CAR PARK
2 DANISH GUARD FIGURES
1 JUNIOR READY STEADY COOK TOY COOKING SET
1 PLASTIC TOY BOAT
1 PLASTIC TOY BARBIE PHONE
7 PLASTIC TOY SKITTLES
1 PLASTIC TOY APPLE
1 PLASTIC BLUE AND WHITE LUNCH BOX
1 PLASTIC TOY STEERING WHEEL
1 CRITTERS PLASTIC TOY KEYBOARD
1 PLASTIC TOY HELICOPTER
1 SOFT TOY DINOSAUR
1 SOFT TOY LADYBIRD
1 PERFECT PETS LUNCH SET
1 CORDUROY PURSE
1 PLASTIC TOY FARMHOUSE
1 PLASTIC TOY FIRST AID KIT
1 FROG SOFT TOY
2 BASEBALL CAPS
1 GOLFER'S WHISKY SET
1 BAG OF FOAM HAIR CURLERS
1 BAG OF ASSORTED WRITING PENS
1 PLASTIC TOY POTTY
1 SOFT TOY GOAT

1 PLASTIC TOY BATH
2 TABLE TENNIS BATS
1 PLASTIC TOY SPADE
1 BAG OF VARIOUS PLASTIC PIECES
1 KNITTED BABY HAT
1 PLASTIC BABY ACTIVITY HOUSE
1 SOFT TOY DINOSAUR
1 KNITTED TOY SCARECROW
1 PLASTIC TOY CASTLE GATE
1 PLASTIC TOY TARGET
1 WIRE CAGE
7 WOODEN DRAWERS WITH METAL HANDLES
14 JUNIOR OXFORD ENCYCLOPAEDIA BOOKS
1 WOODEN SHOESHINE BOX
1 WOODEN DRAWER WITH VARIOUS PAPERS
1 WOODEN AND METAL FOLDING TABLE
2 POLAROID CAMERAS
4 PAINTING STICKS
3 TROLLEY WHEELS
1 METAL CHAIN
1 KITCHEN TIMER
12 TRANSFORMER LEADS
2 WOODEN BENCHES
5 EAR WARMERS
5 PAIRS OF PROTECTIVE GOGGLES
1 BUNCH OF STRING
1 WOODEN TABLE
1 FOLDING WOODEN GARDEN TABLE
2 WOODEN TRESTLE LEGS
1 WOODEN DOOR WITH MISSING WINDOWS
1 FOLDING MUSIC STAND
1 BROKEN SUNLAMP
8 METAL POLES OF VARIOUS HEIGHTS
1 WHITE FOLDING WOODEN GARDEN TABLE
1 DARK BROWN WOODEN SUITCASE
2 METAL SHELVING UNITS
2 CIRCULAR SAWS
1 SANYO VCR
1 OSCILLOSCOPE
1 CLOCKING-IN MACHINE
2 MACROPAC 2.5 SERIES 5 ELECTRONIC BOXES
1 MIXING DESK
1 WHITE PLASTIC FAN
1 DARTBOARD
1 BROKEN GABRIELE 25 TYPEWRITER
1 BLACK SEWING MACHINE
1 PORTABLE TYPEWRITER
1 SINGER 769 WHITE PLASTIC SEWING MACHINE
1 WHITE ELECTRONIC TYPEWRITER
1 GREEN METAL SEWING MACHINE
1 TOY DRUM SET
1 VISCOUNT GREY METAL SEWING MACHINE
1 PLASTIC BOX OF RUSTY TOOLS
1 ADLER GREY METAL TYPEWRITER
1 XEROX 6015 ELECTRONIC TYPEWRITER
1 WOODEN SHELVING UNIT
1 GAS HEATER
1 ELECTRIC HAND SANDER
1 LIGHTING TRANSFORMER
1 NEON TRANSFORMER AND SANDER BOX
1 BROTHER TYPEWRITER
7 PLASTIC HULA HOOPS
2 PLASTIC 'HAZARDOUS AREA' SIGNS
1 LETTER FROM NATWEST BANK TO TOMOKO TAKAHASHI
1 CARROT'S CANNY CAPTION GAME
3 GO FOR BROKE BOARD GAMES
1 EYEWITNESS CHILDREN'S ORGANISER
1 SANTA TEDDY BEAR
1 SUPER GHTER GAME
2 JUNIOR MEDICAL KITS
1 BABY BIRD GAME
1 MAGIC WAND GAME
1 THIS GAME IS WONKERS GAME
1 COLOMINO GAME
1 SPIELESAMMLING 400 GAME
1 TOY MOUNTAIN BIKE
1 BOX OF TOY WINEGLASSES
1 WOODEN HOOP GAME
1 KEYWORD BOARD GAME
1 BAG OF WOODEN COUNTERS
1 JUNIOR DRIVER TOY SOLDIERS AND VEHICLE
1 TOY POOL TABLE
1 JAPANESE SIGN
1 PLASTIC TOY BIKE
2 PICK-UP STICKS GAMES
1 HOME SWEET LULLABY TOY STEREO WITH DOLLS
1 RADICAL CHECKERS ELECTRONIC GAME
1 MATCHBOX CAR
2 BUG'S LIFE PLASTIC TOY BUGS
1 PLASTIC TOY MOBILE PHONE

1 PLASTIC SINK AND CUTLERY SET
1 SET SWITZERLAND TOURIST CARDS
1 SET PINGU THE PENGUIN ALPHABET CARDS
2 SETS OF PLAYING CARDS
1 HORSE JIGSAW PUZZLE
1 PLASTIC BANANA
1 PLASTIC TOY VEHICLE
1 PLASTIC MODEL RADIO CONTROL TOY CAR
1 NECCHI PLASTIC SEWING MACHINE
1 NURSERY RHYMES JIGSAW
1 BROKEN SECTION OF CAST CONCRETE
1 TABULA THE ROMAN BOARD GAME
1 GUESS WHO? BOARD GAME
1 COMPUTER MONITOR
1 RHINO RUSH BOARD GAME
1 FAMILY FORTUNES BOARD GAME
1 BATTLE OF BRITAIN BOARD GAME
1 JUNIOR SCRABBLE BOARD GAME
1 GENIUS BOARD GAME
1 THE NEWS FROM THE BBC BOARD GAME
1 GHOST CASTLE GAME
1 GO FOR IT BOARD GAME
1 BIENEN SPIEL GAME
1 WHO IS IT? GAME
1 4-IN-1 ELECTRIC EXPERIMENT SET
1 TOY AIR GUN
1 JAPANESE CARD GAME
1 TRUE OR FALSE GAME
1 PLASTIC CHILDREN'S TELEPHONE ACTIVITY SET
1 SCUBA SNOOPY SOFT TOY
1 PLASTIC TOY RADIO
1 JAR OF PLASTIC GUN PELLETS
1 BRAID EXPRESS BRAIDING MACHINE
1 KER-PLUNK GAME
1 FRUITY BUGS GAME
1 WIGGLY WORMS GAME
1 EXPLORE EUROPE GAME
1 CHILD'S PLAY MAT
1 RUCKSACK WITH TOY FOOD INSIDE
1 APPLE KEYBOARD
1 BROKEN OLYMPIA TYPEWRITER COVER
1 PLASTIC PLUTO DISNEY TOY
2 MCDONALD'S HAPPY MEAL TOYS
1 PLASTIC TOY STORY DOG FIGURE
1 TOY STORY COWBOY FIGURE
1 PLASTIC HORSE FROM MCDONALD'S HAPPY MEAL
1 TOY FIGURE WITH WIND-UP BOW TIE
1 PLASTIC TOY STORY TOY FIGURE
1 SOFT TOY PENGUIN
1 PLASTIC MICKEY MOUSE FIGURE
1 MCDONALD'S FRENCH FRIES WIND-UP TOY
1 TOY STORY COWGIRL FIGURE
1 MCDONALD'S DRINK WIND-UP TOY
1 ELECTRIC TOY STORY FIGURE
2 BEADED WOMEN'S PURSES
1 MCDONALD'S ICE CREAM WIND-UP TOY
1 MCDONALD'S HAMBURGER WIND-UP TOY
1 SEASHELL
1 PLASTIC LASSO
4 SETS OF DUTCH PLAYING CARDS
5 SETS OF MINIATURE PLAYING CARDS
3 BUNDLES OF COCKTAIL STICKS
2 BIC PENS
1 MINIATURE TOY SOLDIER
1 BROKEN METAL OLIVETTI TYPEWRITER
1 LITTLE TIKES GIRL'S TOY BIKE
1 FLYING SAUCER GAME
1 PINK OFFICE CHAIR
1 BOX OF ASSORTED METAL SPANNERS
1 BLUE OFFICE CHAIR
1 SUNBEAM ELECTRIC GRILL
1 METAL BUCKET
2 PLASTIC TOY TIPPER TRUCKS
1 METAL ROD
1 CARBON COPY MACHINE
1 SILVER REED 500 PORTABLE TYPEWRITER
1 PLASTIC TOY FIRE ENGINE
3 PLASTIC BUCKETS
1 BEDSIDE LAMP WITH BROKEN LAMPSHADE
1 BUCKET OF METAL TOOLS
1 PLASTIC YELLOW TOY PRAM
1 BROKEN PLASTIC TOY TRACTOR
2 BULLDOZER TOYS
1 PLASTIC ENGINEERING TRUCK
1 PLASTIC TRANSFORMER TOY
1 BOX OF TRANSFER SHEETS AND CARBON PAPER
2 SOFT TOY CARS
2 PLASTIC TOY CARS
1 WOODEN TOY TRAILER
1 RUBIK'S CUBE

1 PLASTIC TOY TIPPER TRUCK
1 BOB THE BUILDER CANDY DISPENSER
2 SNOWPLOUGHS
1 WATER COOLER
1 TOY JCB
1 TIPPER TRUCK
1 RED TOY STEAMROLLER
1 TODDLERS' ACTIVITY SET
2 NOT-FALL CAR BOXED GAME
1 BRIEFCASE
1 SET OF HAIR BANDS
1 GAME OF KNOWLEDGE BOXED GAME
1 MINIATURE TABLE TENNIS TABLE
1 HELICOPTER
1 PLASTIC TREE
1 LUNCH BOX SHAPED LIKE A TRUCK
1 KINDER MEMORY BOXED GAME
1 WORTIFIX BOXED GAME
1 TRIO BOXED GAME
1 SNIP SNAP BOXED GAME
1 INTERLOCKING PUZZLE
20 MIRROR PLATES
1 BROKEN CROWBAR
3 SPRAY CANS
2 PAIRS OF GLOVES
1 BROKEN PIPE
2 LENGTHS OF 40 METRE KITELINE
1 RED-AND-BLACK TEMPLATE TOOL
1 WINDOW FIXING KIT
1 DISPLAY BOARD
1 SIGN IN SHAPE OF BLUE ARROW
1 PORTABLE VACUUM CLEANER
1 WIRE
2 ROLLS OF WOODEN FENCING
37 WOODEN CHILDREN'S CHAIRS
2 PLASTIC CHILDREN'S CHAIRS
1 TABLE TENNIS TABLE
1 METAL CARRIER
1 AXION COMPUTER MONITOR
3 SPADES
3 PITCHFORKS
1 OLIVETTI TYPEWRITER
1 BASKETBALL NET WITH BACKBOARD
9 PLASTIC CHAIRS
1 NETBALL
1 BUCKET
1 PIANO STOOL
1 GUILLOTINE
5 WIRE CAGES
2 COMPUTER KEYBOARDS
1 FILING CABINET
1 GARDEN HOSE DISPENSER
1 EXHIBITION CRATE
1 GRASS EDGE TRIMMER
CARPENTRY TOOLS
4 WOODEN SHELVES
1 FISHING NET APPROX 2 METRES
1 TOOL BOX WITH ASSORTED RUSTY OLD TOOLS
2 SINGER ELECTRIC SEWING MACHINES
1 PLASTIC BASE TO BASKETBALL HOOP
1 CRESTA SEWING MACHINE
2 SINGER SEWING MACHINES
2 PORTABLE TYPEWRITERS
1 SINGER SEWING MACHINE
1 SCRAPER
3 BOXES OF TOOLS
1 TOOL BOX
1 BUCKET OF SPANNERS
1 BOX OF SPANNERS
1 WOODEN CLAMP
1 ELECTRIC TYPEWRITER
2 WOODEN GARDEN GATES
1 METAL TRUNK
1 REMINGTON TYPEWRITER
1 CLAMP
1 BROTHER ELECTRIC EP20 TYPEWRITER
1 TYPEWRITER
CANVAS WITH ROPE
1 WOODEN DRAWER
1 BIKE RACK
1 ELECTRIC TYPEWRITER
1 TROLLEY
1 JIGSAW
1 ELECTRIC FAN
1 TOOL BOX
1 PLASTIC KETTLE
1 TOOL BOX
1 ELECTRIC SINGER SEWING MACHINE
1 SEWING MACHINE IN GREEN CASE
1 SUITCASE

ASSORTED DRILL BITS
1 FRISTER AND ROSSMON SEWING MACHINE
1 DINGY PUMP
4 TYPEWRITER PARTS
1 ELLA SEWING MACHINE
1 BOX OF CABLES
1 CONSUL TYPEWRITER
1 JONES SEWING MACHINE
ASSORTED GARDEN HOSES
1 SANCTIO DUALUX 2000 H PROJECTOR IN BOX
1 SEWING MACHINE PEDAL
METAL CABLES
1 KNITTING MACHINE
1 DOLEX PROJECTOR
GARDEN CUTTERS
2 CURVED METAL POLES
1 TOOL TRAY
1 PAIR OF PINK FLIPPERS
3 WHITE TELEPHONES
1 YELLOW BRICK
1 GREY TELEPHONE
4 YELLOW METAL TIPPER TRUCKS
1 YELLOW METAL DIGGER
1 PHONE BOOK
1 CROWBAR
1 PACK OF STEEL WOOL
1 BOX OF PLASTIC CLOCKS
1 METAL COAT HANGER
1 CLIP FRAME WITHOUT CLIPS
1 PLIABLE CONDUIT
1 NO SMOKING SIGN
1 DOOR LOCKED SIGN
1 PAD OF GRAPH PAPER
1 PIERCED COPPER PLANT POT
1 GREEN METAL FIRST AID BOX
2 PLASTIC AMBULANCES
2 PENNY WHISTLES
1 SPACEMAN TOY
5 PLANT TRAYS
1 FUJI FILM
1 FOOTBALL
VENETIAN BLINDS
1 TOY HACKSAW
1 SET OF TOY MICRO MACHINE ARMY MEN
1 BICYCLE LOCK
1 RAT TRAP
1 PACK OF PENS
1 EMPTY WOODEN BOX
1 SET OF EMERGENCY VEHICLE TOYS
1 BOX OF METAL CLAMPS AND TOOLS
1 PLASTIC METAL DETECTOR
1 RED FIRE BELL
1 STRESS BALL
1 CRICKET GLOVE
CANVAS WITH METAL HOOPS
1 RED PLASTIC CONTAINER
2 EMPTY FILES
1 SET OF TOOLS
ESTATE AGENT STATIONERY
2 SPONGES
1 RED CAR
1 THE DISTINCTIVE TWO...IN AUDIO TAPE
2 FRUSTRATION GAMES
1 CHUMP THE CHIMP GAME
1 OCTOPUS WHIRL GAME
1 POKEMON GAME
1 SORRY BOXED GAME
1 WILDLIFE BOXED GAME
1 LOS ANGELES ANGELS BASKETBALL GAME
1 SUM-IT: THE GURRENCY GAME GAME
1 WIGGLY WORMS GAME
1 TENSION GAME
1 TRANSPORT: 3 IN A BOX GAME
1 SCRABBLE FOR JUNIORS GAME
1 DARE GAME
1 NUMBER MASTER MIND GAME
1 HANGMAN GAME
1 BUCKAROO GAME
1 WHAT? GAME
1 GRAND PRIX GAME
1 SCRABBLE GAME
1 NEIGHBOURS GAME
1 BATTERY-OPERATED PLASTIC GUN
1 INSPECTOR HIGGINS GAME
1 PAYDAY GAME
1 POP UP PIRATE GAME
1 WHAT TIME IS IT? GAME
1 ANIMALS JIGSAW
1 CONSTRUCTION SET
1 THOMAS THE TANK ENGINE JIGSAW

1 KNIGHTS IN THE SKY COMPUTER GAME
1 SAVE THE ANIMALS GAME
1 QUIZ BOXED GAME
1 FLEAS ON FRED GAME
1 PERFECT PRESS BEAD MAKING GAME
1 DIZZY DINOSAUR GAME
1 HANGMAN GAME
1 SILLY FACES GAME
1 THE LONDON GAME
1 MOUSE TRAP BOXED GAME
1 CRAYOLA DESIGNER KIT BOXED GAME
1 IMITATION LEATHER SUITCASE
1 FAMILY FORTUNES BOARD GAME
1 JITTERS GAME
1 YAHTZEE GAME
1 DISNEY'S HAPPY EVER AFTER GAME
1 HIDE AND SEEK GAME
1 WRITE START GAME
1 WORD POOL GAME
1 LAUNDRY BAG
1 JIGSAW
1 HI Q GAME
1 VIKING JIGSAW
2 SETS OF PLAYING CARDS
1 PAIR BEARDS GAME
1 MAH-JONG GAME
1 STAD LAND FLUSS GAME
1 SUPER SNAKES AND LADDERS GAME
1 FASHION WHEEL DESIGNER KIT
1 COCONUT DROP GAME
1 MAH-JONG GAME
1 MID-LIFE CRISIS GAME
1 RAPID FIRE BALL GAME
1 SEALED WITH A KISS GAME
1 JIGSAW
1 PACK OF PLAYING CARDS
1 THE PARTY GAME BOARD GAME
1 TOY TOOL SET
1 TOY BUILDING SET
1 TOY KITCHEN SET
1 AIR HOCKEY GAME GAME
1 TOY BLENDER SET
ASSORTED BALLS
1 TRANSPARENT GLASS JAR
1 POP'N'HOP GAME
1 LIGHT FANTASTIC GAME
5 TOY MOUNTAIN BIKES
1 ELECTRONIC EXPERIMENT SET
1 JIGSAW
1 SOFT TOY ELEPHANT
1 VAN
1 RED FIRE TRUCK
MULTICOLOURED PLASTIC SHAPES
1 FISHER-PRICE PLASTIC BOAT
1 PURPLE-AND-GREEN BOAT
1 BOULES SET
1 TOY TELEVISION
1 TOY INFLATABLE DINGY
1 TOY HANDYMAN TOOL BELT
1 TOY CLAMP
1 STAINED GLASS SOLDERING IRON
1 DISCO LAMP
8 PERSPEX DISPLAY STANDS
3 COMPUTER MONITORS
1 PRINTER
1 REEL OF CABLE
1 CONTAINER
3 PERSPEX SHEETS
1 FOAM SHEET
10 ELECTRIC CABLES, VARIOUS LENGTHS
1 GREEN AV LEAD
1 WOODEN BANISTER
4 DISPLAY TABLES PAINTED WHITE
4 PERSPEX DISPLAY CASE TOPS
2 ELECTRIC CABLES
4 POWER LEADS FOR MICROPHONES
25 ACOUSTIC PANEL JOINTS
3 IN/OUT CABLES
6 PERSPEX BOXES
1 POWER CABLE
16 WHITE SHELF-BRACKETS
1 YELLOW POWER CABLE
4 GREY SHELF-BRACKETS
ELECTRIC WIRE COLOURED PINK
4 TRANSFORMER LEADS
1 VENETIAN BLIND
3 OFFICE DESK-LAMPS
9 KETTLE LEADS
6 MICROPHONE LEADS
1 SPEAKER CABLE

1 MICROPHONE
1 GREY POWER CABLE
1 SPEAKER CABLE
10 METAL POLES
13 METRE ELECTRIC CABLE
1 MODEL OF NORTH GALLERY SPACE
1 VOLTAGE CONTROLLER
2 ROLLS OF ELECTRIC CABLE
3 COMPAQ COMPUTER KEYBOARDS
2 HALOGEN LAMPS
1 REEL OF BLUE ROPE
3 GATEWAY COMPUTER KEYBOARDS
2 WHITE MDF PLINTHS
3 CLIP-ON SPOTLIGHTS
1 FAN
1 VACUUM CLEANER
1 WHITE MDF SHELF
1 TELEPHONE CABLE
1 COMPUTER KEYBOARD IN BOX
1 WHITE ELECTRIC FAN
1 COMPUTER KEYBOARD
16 TRANSFORMERS WITH LEADS
1 TROLLEY WITH WHITE DRAWERS
1 DICTAPHONE HEADSET
33 KETTLE LEADS
1 SONY MINI-SPEAKER
6 CABLES FOR MODEMS
1 POWER CABLE
1 POWER CABLE FOR COMPUTER
7 YELLOW CABLES FOR MODEMS
1 TELEPHONE SOCKET DOUBLE ADAPTOR IN ORIGINAL PACKAGING
4 WOODEN TRESTLE LEGS
2 TELEPHONE EXTENSION LEADS
4 GREY CABLES FOR MODEMS
1 RED PLASTIC BUCKET
300 YELLOW PING PONG BALLS
2 SETS OF FAIRY LIGHTS SHAPED AS SOFT FRUITS
2 METAL TOYS
1 MAGIC 8 BALL
1 SPACE EXPLORATION TOY
1 COOL TOOL ADVENTURES TOY
2 SWIMSUITS FOR BARBIE DOLL
2 BARBIE PICNIC SETS
1 BARBIE CAKE MIXING SET
1 BARBIE KITCHEN SET
2 YELLOW AND RED PLASTIC TOW TRUCKS
1 RED AND YELLOW FIRE ENGINE
1 METAL LOCK
2 BARBIE DENIM JACKETS
1 PAIR OF BARBIE DOLL STILETTOS
1 PLASTIC POLICE CAR
1 YELLOW AND WHITE PLASTIC CRANE
1 TOY HOVERCRAFT
1 YELLOW TOW TRUCK
1 YELLOW BOOMERANG
1 MEASURING TOOL
1 TOMBOLA SET
ASSORTED MILITARY FIGURES
1 BLUE PLANE
1 GREEN ALLIGATOR
1 TOY FORKLIFT IN BOX
1 BOX OF ASSORTED TOYS
1 YELLOW DIGGER
1 GREY PLASTIC TOY GUN
1 TOY COFFEE MAKER
1 MINIATURE GOLF SET
1 PENCIL SHARPENER SHAPED LIKE FILM CAMERA
1 PUZZLE
1 GYMKANA BOXED GAME
1 MONOPOLY BOXED GAME
1 JIGSAW WITH CAR MOTIF
1 BAG OF FOAM LETTERS AND NUMBERS
1 TRACEY ISLAND TOY
1 GAME OF MARBLES
2 PLEASE DO NOT TOUCH SIGNS
200 FISH-SHAPED SOY SAUCE DISPENSERS
1 CINDY DOLL IN PACKAGING
1 PLASTIC DRILL
1 TABLE SAW
1 CALCULATOR PEN
3 ROLLERBALL PEN SETS
7 TOY SEMI TRUCKS
1 SCREWDRIVER
1 TRUCK-SHAPED CLOCKS
1 CARRIER BAG FULL OF SOCKS AND SHOES
10 BALLOONS AND PUMP
1 PLASTIC TOOL CASE AND TOOLS
1 TOY FIREMAN'S HELMET
1 SPONGE FOOTBALL
1 KEY CHAIN

1 FAKE LEATHER PURSE
1 SET OF PLASTIC KEYS
ASSORTED BLACK PAPER SHAPES
1 PLASTIC DINOSAUR
1 TOY SHELL GAS STATION
1 PLASTIC KICKING HORSE
1 SPONGE BASKETBALL
1 CLOCK WITH ANIMAL PATTERN
1 KEY CHAIN WITH VIEW MASTER
1 KEY CHAIN SHAPED LIKE A PLANE
ASSORTED JINGLE BELLS
30 SETS OF PLAYING CARDS
1 MEASURING AND RULER SET
1 FOOTBALL GAME
1 PLASTIC SKATEBOARD
40 SECTIONS OF ELECTRIC RACETRACK
1 STEERING WHEEL LOCK
1 FILTER WALLET
3 GENERATION GIRL MAGAZINE LEAFLETS
1 MY WORKSHOP TOY
2 BOWLING SETS
1 MINI SKEEBALL GAME
ASSORTED BOOKS ON CARD GAMES
1 50-GAMES BOX BOARD GAME
1 STRATEGO BOARD GAME
1 MELTED CAR LIGHT
1 TOY FIREMAN'S HAT
1 BROKEN COMPACT RADIO
1 PLASTIC TOY GUN
1 BAG OF MARBLES
1 BRASS TOY GUN
1 TOY MOTORCYCLE
1 WOODEN RACKET
1 TOY MERCEDES BENZ
2 INCOMPLETE BATTLESHIP GAMES
4 PLASTIC TRAYS
1 SPANISH DOLL
2 SOFT TENNIS RACKETS
15 SHEETS OF BOOK PAGES
6 GAME BOARDS
1 JAR OF PLAYDOUGH
1 PLASTIC SPHERE
1 SUITCASE
1 TOY RIFLE
1 ORANGE CHESS FIGURE
1 GREEN-AND-BLUE PLASTIC TOY BUS
3 RED WOODEN SKIPPING ROPE HANDLES
1 BAG OF ASSORTED PLASTIC GAME PIECES
1 WOODEN RATTLE
1 BLACK CROWBAR
1 PAIR OF METAL PLIERS
1 GREY PLASTIC OFFICE TRAY
3 ROLLS GAFFER TAPE
2 ROLLS MASKING TAPE
15 ASSORTED MARKERS
1 GREY STANLEY KNIFE
1 RED STAPLE GUN
1 SCREWDRIVER
1 YELLOW KNEEPAD
1 ROLL OF WHITE OFFICE LABELS
1 ROLL OF RED-AND-WHITE HAZARD TAPE
1 PLASTIC ELECTRIC TIMER
1 PADDING KNIFE
100 BLACK CABLE TIES
200 WHITE CABLE TIES
50 PLASTIC BLUE AND RED GAME COUNTERS
1 METAL CLEANING BRUSH
4 ASSORTED MARKING PENS
5 ASSORTED KEY RINGS
1 CARRIER BAG WITH ASSORTED ADAPTOR CABLES
40 ASSORTED KITCHEN UTENSILS
1 BLUE-AND-WHITE JAPANESE HANDKERCHIEF
17 REMOTE CONTROLS FOR TOY CARS
200 COWBOY AND INDIAN TOY FIGURES
3 PLASTIC REMOTE CONTROLLED CARS
1 MICRO MACHINE SKULL ON WHEELS TOY
2 METAL KNITTING MACHINE PARTS
1 PLASTIC TOY CALCULATOR
1 WALKIE-TALKIE SHAPED SWEET DISPENSER
1 PLASTIC PURPLE OFFICE TRAY
1 TRAVEL BATTLESHIP GAME
14 FOOTBALL PLAYER FIGURES
1 GREY PLASTIC CASH REGISTER SCREEN WITH LEAD
VARIOUS PARTS OF ELECTRIC CASH REGISTER
10 METRES OF ROPE
1 WHITE PLASTIC CASH DRAWER
1 CANVAS IKEA BAG
1 INCOMPLETE CAR RACING GAME
1 PLASTIC TOY TANK WITH REMOTE CONTROL
1 PLASTIC TRAFFIC LIGHT RATTLE

1 PRO-ACTION FOOTBALL SCOREBOARD
1 PLASTIC MINIGOLF CLUB
1 DARTBOARD
1 PLASTIC START GATE
1 MANUAL SINGER SEWING MACHINE
1 PAIR PLASTIC HANDCUFFS
1 BOX OF DOMINOES
1 INCOMPLETE JUNIOR DOCTOR TOY SET
1 PLASTIC MINIATURE POOL TABLE
1 PLASTIC STENCIL
1 WOODEN GAME WITH 10 PLASTIC TRUCKS INSIDE
54 PLAYING CARDS
1 PLASTIC TOY TRACTOR
1 TOY SHELL LORRY
1 JUNIOR ELECTRO GAME SET
1 RUSTY METAL GARBAGE CAN
1 METAL TAPE DISPENSER
1 USED LIGHT BULB
14 ASSORTED MAGNETIC SIGNS
2 VIDEO TAPES IN PLASTIC PACKAGING
10 AUDIO CASSETTE TAPES
1 TOY TRANSPORT TRAILER
1 MARBLE GAME
2 INCOMPLETE TRAVEL CHESS GAMES
1 PLASTIC TOY COMPASS
2 PAINT BRUSHES
1 BAG OF METAL RATCHETS
3 SCREWDRIVERS
2 SILVER PLASTIC KEYBOARD COVERS
1 PUZZLE BOOK
1 20TH CENTURY ILLUSTRATED SPORTS BOOK
1 BICYCLE REPAIR MANUAL
3 ACTIVITY BOOKS
1 SHEET BOB THE BUILDER GIFT WRAP
2 SKETCHBOOKS
1 WILLIERS BROTHERS FURNITURE BROCHURE
1 CLOTH SAMPLE BOOK
1 PAINT SAMPLE BOOK
1 EVERGREEN DESIGNER FLOWERS CATALOGUE
1 MEN AT WORK CATALOGUE
50 ASSORTED COCKTAIL STICKS
50 PAPER CLOAKROOM TICKETS
1 HADLEY MARQUEES BROCHURE
2 EVEREADY HIRE CENTRE PRICE LIST
1 ARTISTS SUPPLIES CATALOGUE (1998)
1 GREENHAM CATALOGUE
1 KINKO PRICE LIST
1 CAMDEN FURNITURE CATALOGUE
1 LONDON GRAPHIC CENTRE CATALOGUE
1 OPTIKINETIKS CATALOGUE
1 FABRIC AND VINYL SAMPLE BOOK
1 PLASTIC CONTAINER
2 PHOTO BOOKS
1 BLUE PLASTIC TYPEWRITER COVER
1 TOY PICKUP TRUCK
1 BOX WOODEN BUILDING BLOCKS
1 BLACK PLASTIC PENCIL CASE
1 RED PALLET GUN
2 JAPANESE TOY TELEPHONES
2 METAL CHAINS
1 SCUBA DIVER TOY FIGURE
1 DJ SUPER SCRATCH TOY
1 TOY PIANO AND PIANO PLAYER
1 MY PARTY PLASTIC PLAY SET
1 PAIR METAL HANDCUFFS
1 BAG OF ASSORTED PUZZLE PIECES
1 SILVER PLASTIC CROWN
1 PLASTIC TOY DINOSAUR
1 PLASTIC TOY POLICE TRUCK
1 SATURN'S RING GAME
1 BLUE-AND-RED PLASTIC YO-YO
10 SETS OF PLAYING CARDS
1 STAPLE WIZARD TOY STAPLER
2 PLASTIC GLOW-IN-THE-DARK TOY SHARKS
1 RED PLASTIC RACING CAR
1 TIME BRICK COMPUTER GAME
1 PLASTIC PIECE OF TOY SPACE ROCKET
1 YELLOW METAL TOY SPEEDBOAT
ASSORTED PLASTIC TOY TOOLS AND CHEST
41 MINIATURE TOY VANS
1 WOODEN BIRD WHISTLE
1 BAG OF WHALE- AND SHARK-SHAPED PENCIL TOPS
19 MINIATURE PLASTIC TOY TRACTORS
12 PLASTIC TOY SHARKS
1 OLLIE THE OSTRICH SOFT TOY
1 GREY SOFT TOY SHARK
1 PLASTIC SHARK-SHAPED STAPLER
1 MULTICOLOURED RUBBER BALL
1 SQUEAKY TOY
1 PLASTIC TOY SPACE SHUTTLE

1 PLASTIC TOY SPACE BUGGY
1 YELLOW SOFT TOY DINOSAUR
1 BLUE RUBBER TOY FROG
1 PLASTIC WATER GUN
40 MINIATURE TOY SPACEMEN FIGURES
1 TOY MOUNTAIN BIKE WITH SPARE WHEELS
1 ROLL BLUE COTTON THREAD
1 PINK PLASTIC CONTAINER
1 HANDMADE BLACK-AND-WHITE TEDDY BEAR
1 PLASTIC TOY PAN
1 INCOMPLETE WOODEN PUZZLE
1 WOODEN HAIRBRUSH
1 PLASTIC PINK-AND-PURPLE PEARL NECKLACE
1 STRAW BASKET
1 BROKEN BOB THE BUILDER WRIST WATCH
1 BLACK LEATHER WALLET
1 SOFT TOY HORSE SHAPED LIKE A BOWLING PIN
1 PURPLE SOFT TOY HIPPO
2 PLASTIC MAZE GAMES
1 MINIATURE METAL GODDESS HEAD
1 GLASS MINIATURE TEA TABLE
2 MINIATURE DUTCH WOODEN SHOES
1 METAL CANDLEHOLDER
1 WOODEN WATER PIPE
1 YELLOW ELEPHANT RATTLE SOFT TOY
1 ORANGE PLASTIC GOLF BALL
200 ASSORTED BUILDING BLOCKS
1 PLASTIC WIND-UP CAR
1 YELLOW WORKMAN'S GLOVE
1 BROKEN ALARM CLOCK
2 WOODEN SQUARE BRACKETS
1 INCOMPLETE MEMORY CARD GAME
1 YELLOW SPONGE
1 PLASTIC TOY CLOCK
1 PART OF LEATHER CASE
1 RUSTY METAL CALLIPER
5 MICROSCOPES
228 GLASS TEST TUBES
1 METALLIC AND PLASTIC MOULD
1 BUNSEN BURNER
1 FLASK CLAMP
1 FLASK HOLDER
1 PAIR OF SAFETY GOGGLES
1 POWDER MEASURER
2 CHINA PESTLES
1 SCALPEL HOLDER
1 PAIR SCISSORS
1 TEST TUBE BASE
10 GLASS COLLECTION BOTTLES
1 PLASTIC FUNNEL
1 GLASS FUNNEL
1 MEASURING FLASK
3 FLUORESCENT FLASKS
1 PLASTIC YELLOW LIGHT GLOBE
33 FLASKS
1 CHEMISTRY GLOBE
1 YELLOW PLASTIC BUCKET
6 BLACK KETTLE LEADS
1 BAG OF SORTED LEGO PIECES
1 PINK-AND-WHITE STRIPED HULA HOOP
2 SMALL PINK PLASTIC CHAIRS
1 WOODEN TROLLEY
1 ROCK ROLL GAME
1 BAG OF PLASTIC TOY CARS AND TRAINS
1 GREEN PLASTIC TOY BUGGY
1 BAG OF CLEAR MARBLES
1 PLASTIC TOY SHARK
4 LARGE BLACK CROW ANIMAL FIGURES
1 EMPTY THE SEAFARER JIGSAW PUZZLE BOX
1 BOX OF CORONET DARTS
1 BOX OF WOODEN CHESS PIECES
2 BOXES OF PLASTIC TOY AEROPLANES
1 MINIATURE SNAP CARD GAME
1 TOMY POCKET RACING GAME
1 AFTER EIGHT DRAUGHTS PIECES
1 BOX OF DOMINOES
1 WOODEN CUBE PUZZLE
1 CROQUET SET
1 BOX OF KINDER TOYS
1 BOX OF WOODEN DRAUGHTS
1 BOX OF WOODEN CHESS PIECES
2 BOXES OF 16TH CENTURY BOATS AND PLASTIC CARS
1 BOX OF PAINTED PLASTIC CARS
1 BOX OF CHRISTMAS CRACKER TYPE GAMES
1 TOP MONKEY GAME
1 BOX OF ASSORTED GAME BOARDS
3 INCOMPLETE JIGSAW BOXES
1 GREEN CANVAS BAG
1 GREEN WOODEN TROLLEY
1 GREEN WOODEN PIN BALL GAME

6 DARTS
3 DART SETS
1 RED METAL TOY FIRE ENGINE
1 YELLOW METAL TOY FARM VEHICLE
81 WALKING COMPASSES
1 BAG ASSORTED DART FLIGHTS
1 RED METAL TOY FERRARI
1 HOVIS METAL TOY DELIVERY VAN
48 ASSORTED JIGSAW PUZZLES
20 VHS TAPES
1 WOODEN BOX
1 NUIRHEAD METAL RADIO TRANSMITTER
1 KELVIN HUGHES METAL GRAPH MACHINE
1 PLASTIC ELECTRICAL FAN
1 METAL ABO METER
1 MAGIMIX FOOD BLENDER
1 CAR BATTERY BOOSTER PACK
2 LIGHT BOXES
1 EXTERNAL LAMP
1 BLACK LEATHER BRIEFCASE
1 WOODEN CRATE WITH PLASTIC FLOWERS INSIDE
3 RUSTY METAL PETROL CANS
1 LEATHER AND WOODEN CHAIR
1 RANCHO PLAYHOUSE
1 GLASS VITRINE
1 PLASTIC BOX OF METAL SCRAPS
1 BROKEN BUTTERFLY NET
1 KLASSIK FLOOR CLEANER
1 PLASTIC TOY STABLES
1 FRUSTRATION BOARD GAME
1 BAG OF ASSORTED PLASTIC COLOURED TOYS
1 BOX OF TIDDLYWINKS
7 VARIOUS SOFT TOY ANIMALS
1 PLASTIC TOY STORY VILLAIN FIGURE
1 PLASTIC TOY STORY BUZZ LIGHTYEAR TOY FIGURE
1 ROBOT DOG TOY
1 RED PLASTIC TOY SPORTS CAR
1 BLUE PLASTIC TOY LORRY
1 PLASTIC TOY TEA SET
1 PLASTIC TOY FIRST AID KIT
1 PINK PLASTIC LORRY
1 CLOTHES BASKET
1 MUSTAFA HAMSTER TOY
1 PLASTIC DRILL
14 VARIOUS HATS
1 PLASTIC TELEPHONE
2 PLASTIC TOY WALKIE-TALKIES
1 CLOCKWORK PLASTIC TOY FISH
1 ELECTRIC GOGGLE TOY
2 PLASTIC TOY TENNIS RACKETS
1 ARMBAND
1 CLEAR PLASTIC SHOWER CAP
1 BLACK PLASTIC TOY CAR PART
1 SQUARE WICKER BASKET
1 ELECTRIC FAN
1 FUNKY FOOTPRINTS PLASTIC TOY WALKING AID
1 PLASTIC TOOL BOX
1 PAIR RED CHILD'S WELLINGTON BOOTS
1 INFLATABLE BARBIE SWIMMING RING
1 TIGGER INFLATABLE TOY
1 FATHER CHRISTMAS TOY
1 METAL LAMP
1 MERMAID TAILS AUDIO TAPE
1 GREY TOY GUN BARREL
1 WHITE METAL CLOTHES HORSE
1 BLUE WOODEN MENU BOARD
2 BROKEN FRUIT MACHINE PARTS
1 PLASTIC TOY FAN
1 WASH BAG
1 HI-FI SOFT TOY
1 CHOPPER PATROL PLASTIC MAT
1 BLACK DOG HARNESS
1 PAIR PURPLE IN-LINE SKATES
1 METAL TWEENIES PENCIL CASE
1 HI-FI STEREO
1 GREY TOY MOTORBIKE
1 STRAW LAMPSHADE
1 BLACK SUITCASE WITH ASSORTED STRAPS
1 FISHER-PRICE TOY CASH REGISTER
1 POCKET TOY GOLF GAME
1 GREEN-WHEELED PLASTIC CRATE
1 PLASTIC RATTLE
1 PINK SOFT TOY PIG
1 WOODEN HIPPO
1 BAG ASSORTED KITCHEN ITEMS
1 ELECTRICAL TRANSFORMER
1 BAG OF LARGE LEGO BLOCKS
1 YELLOW TOY ELEPHANT
1 RED PLASTIC TOY TEACUP
1 BLACK DUSTBIN LID

1 CUTLERY RACK
2 PIECES OF BROKEN METAL STEPLADDER
8 PLASTIC DINOSAUR SHAPES
1 SHELLY PLASTIC TOY CAR
1 CLICKING FROG TOY
5 PLASTIC TOY GATES
1 SMALL RED COWBOY HAT
2 TOY FOAM ROLLERS
1 RACING CAR
1 TOY WOODEN DISC
1 KIT COM SPINNING TOP TOY
1 PLASTIC WINDOW
1 WHITE GOLF BALL
1 RED PLASTIC SHAPE
1 BAG OF CHRISTMAS DECORATIONS
3 CHILDREN'S JIGSAW PUZZLES
1 TOY CARGO TOWER
1 GREEN-AND-BLACK TOY TRACTOR
1 PLASTIC PIECE OF CAR TRACK
1 RED PLASTIC TOY WATERING CAN
25 ASSORTED AUDIO CASSETTES
1 LONG-HANDLED GARDEN PITCHFORK
1 YELLOW KNEEPAD
1 MEMO BOARD
1 HOME-MADE SNAKES AND LADDERS BOARD GAME
1 SMALL HAND SAW
1 BOOK
1 SHELF UNIT
1 WOODEN CRATE
1 NAVY BLUE BOBBLE HAT
1 RUSTY CHAIN
1 PACK OF PRESENTATION NOTES
2 SPECIAL DELIVERY BOOKS
1 TRAY OF ASSORTED 12" RECORDS, SOME BROKEN
1 PAIR BLACK LEATHER SHOES
1 CAN OF MR SHEEN
1 BOX PLASTIC TOYS AND TOY CARS
1 ECONOMICS MADE SIMPLE BOOK
1 BAG OF PLASTER
1 METAL SCAFFOLD JOINT
1 THE LEARNING GAME
1 SPEECHLESS GAME
1 PLASTIC TOY VENDING MACHINE
1 MY FIRST BOOK OF WORDS BOOK
1 WHO'S THAT BOOK
1 TOYS BOOK
1 THE NEW COOKERY ENCYCLOPAEDIA
1 ODD JOBS BOOK
1 WHAT'S COOKING BOOK
1 PLASTIC TOY CD PLAYER
1 PLASTIC TOY CONTROL PAD
1 PAIR OF SWIMMING GOGGLES
1 LEGO CHILD'S RUCKSACK WITH TOYS
1 INFANT LEARNING TOY WITHOUT THE PIECES
1 BURGUNDY WALLET
100 TOY CARS
1 BURGUNDY WOMAN'S PURSE
1 ACTION MAN GAME
80-100 GREEN AND RED PLASTIC TOY SOLDIERS
35 ASSORTED PENS
1 BLUE PLASTIC TOY CAR
5 ASSORTED BOOKS
1 RED PEG-HITTING MACHINE
1 THE AMAZING SPACESHIP
1 GREEN PLASTIC TOY VAN
1 WOODEN TOY CAR
1 WOODEN TOY SNAIL CAR
1 REMOTE CONTROL TOY CAR WITHOUT CONTROLLER
1 BLACK PLASTIC TOY CAR
1 PLASTIC PIECE OF CAR TRACK
1 TOY FIRST AID KIT
1 GIRL'S DOLL
1 WHITE PLASTIC VAN
4 BLACK LEATHER CREDIT CARD HOLDERS
1 YELLOW PLASTIC TOY BUS
1 THOMAS THE TANK ENGINE TOY
1 DOLL IN SPANISH NATIONAL DRESS
2 DOLLS IN DUTCH NATIONAL DRESS
1 RED WIND UP MUSICAL BOX
1 SPIRAL ART PLAY SET
1 HAVEN JIGSAW PUZZLE
1 SUPER RACING WIND-UP TOY CAR
40 ASSORTED BROKEN TOYS
1 ORANGE PLASTIC ICE CUBE TRAY
1 ORANGE RATTLE
1 PLASTIC TOY TRAFFIC LIGHTS SET
9 ASSORTED PLASTIC TOY CARS
1 PLASTIC BLUE TROLLEY
1 WOODEN TOY CAR
1 PLASTIC BLUE AND GREEN TOY BOAT

2 RED PLASTIC TOY BRIDGES
1 BAG OF ASSORTED ROAD SIGNS
1 GREEN PLASTIC CUBE
10 ASSORTED JIGSAW PIECES
1 GREY PLASTIC TOY DINOSAUR
6 PLASTIC COCA-COLA BOTTLES
1 PAIR ORANGE GLOVES
1 RED COIN COUNTER
1 GREY CONTAINER WITH MONEY, FOOTBALL AND BOAT
1 BROKEN DIGITAL CLOCK
2 METAL SHELF-BRACKETS
2 RED-AND-BLUE PLASTIC TOY CRANES
2 PLASTIC SPACEMEN AND SPACESHIP JELLY MOULD
2 PAIRS PURPLE-AND-GREEN BABY KNEEPADS
1 SOFT TOY CAMEL
1 SOFT TOY KOALA BEAR
1 TOY LADYBIRD WITH BELL
1 PLASTIC BLACK STALLION TOY
1 BLACKBOARD
1 RED METAL POST OFFICE TROLLEY
1 CARD TABLE WITH DETACHABLE TOP
1 MINIATURE POOL TABLE
2 GREY PROJECTION SCREENS
2 ORANGE METAL SHELF UNITS
1 CAR JACK
1 METAL SILVER CONE LAMPSHADE
1 RED METAL STOP SIGN
1 A4 TIMETABLE IN BROWN FOLDER
1 YELLOW PLASTIC TOOL TRAY
1 PLASTIC NAME BADGE
1 WOODEN FIRE DOOR
1 BOX OF DRINKING GLASSES
2 BLACK PLASTIC TORCHES
1 BLACK HI-FI STEREO
1 METAL DOOR PART
1 WHITE EXTENSION LEAD
3 WHITE TRANSFORMER LEADS
1 METAL OUTDOOR LIGHT
1 PIECE OF PLASTIC FLOOR MOULDING
1 WOODEN PICTURE FRAME
11 HEAVY-DUTY BREATHING MASKS
2 WOODEN BASEBALL BATS
1 BROWN LEATHER BASEBALL GLOVE
1 METAL DOOR LOCK
1 LIGHT BLUE METAL SEWING MACHINE
1 THREADED PIECE OF METAL
1 GARDEN PITCHFORK
2 PLASTIC BUCKETS OF ASSORTED RUSTY TOOLS
1 METAL ARCHITECTURAL DRAWING BOARD
2 BLACK PLASTIC BUILDERS BUCKETS
1 VOLTAGE DIAL WOODEN BOX
2 HANDHELD LAMPS
1 TUBE OF TRACING PAPER
200 SETS OF PLAYING CARDS
1 PORTABLE TYPEWRITER LID
1 CLARKE INDUSTRIAL CHOP SAW
1 BLACK AND GREEN VACUUM CLEANER
2 30 x 20 CM CEMENT PAVING SLABS
1 OUTDOOR BROOM
1 YELLOW PLASTIC ENGINEERING TOY TRUCK
1 PAIR OF GRAVIS TRAINERS
1 ROLL OF MASKING FILM
1 BAG OF PURPLE GLITTER
1 CAN OF HARMONY HAIRSPRAY
1 TIN OF LIQUID WELD
1 TUBE ACRYLIC VARNISH
2 TINS OF BRASSO
1 CAN OF ADHESIVE SPRAY
1 TUBE CRACKLE GLAZE
1 TUBE OF SCUMBLE GLAZE
1 TUBE BLACK ACRYLIC PAINT
1 WIRE COIL
1 HANDFUL ASSORTED SCREWS
1 PINK TRAY
1 STACKABLE BLUE PLASTIC CONTAINER
1 BLACK RACING BICYCLE WITH BACK WHEEL MISSING
1 WOODEN TROLLEY
1 TYPEWRITER WITH EXTERIOR COVER MISSING
1 BROTHER TYPEWRITER
1 OLIVETTI TYPEWRITER
1 METAL UNIT WITH 6 SHELVES
1 PORTABLE PROJECTOR WITH GREY CARRYING CASE
1 BROKEN OLIVETTI TYPEWRITER
1 BLUE VOLTMETER
1 MARCONI AUDIO TESTER
1 HEWLETT PACKARD PRINTER
1 OUT OF CONTROL GAME
1 LIGHT BOX
1 DINGBATS GAME
1 HEDGEHOGS REVENGE GAME

1 PACK OF PAPER MEASURING CUPS
1 CLEAR STAIRCASE SIGN
1 GI JOE GREEN PLASTIC TOY TANK
1 SCALEXTRIC CAR SET
1 EMPTY BROWN METAL BOX
1 MAGNET GAME
1 JAPAN GUIDEBOOK
1 JUNIOR HACKSAW TOY
3 PLASTIC TOY CRANES
1 PRINTED ROLL OF TAPE
1 DISK HOLDER WITH COLOURING PENS
1 NUMBER 10 BILLIARD BALL
1 PAINTBRUSH
6 SOUP CONTAINERS
1 ORANGE METAL FORKLIFT TIPPER TRUCK
2 BINDERS
3 ASSORTED COLOUR MARKER PENS
1 BLUE PLASTIC TRAY
1 TUB OF VASELINE
1 FOOD PROCESSOR WITH BLADES
1 50CM METAL RULER
1 BROWN AND BEIGE 2-DOOR CABINET
1 KINDER ZAUBERSPIELE HARDYS MAGIC SET
1 MID-LIFE CRISIS GAME
1 SNOOKER AND POOL SET
4 KER-PLUNK GAMES
1 POWER PUFF GIRLS GAME
1 BUCKAROO GAME
20 20 QUESTIONS GAME
1 GREEDY GREEN FROG GAME
1 MOUSE TRAP GAME
1 CHAMPION RACING GAME
1 GHOST CASTLE GAME
1 GOOSE BUMPS GAME
1 SNAKES AND LADDERS GAME
1 WHOT GAME
1 GONNA GET YER GAME
1 MOUSE TRAP GAME
1 THERAPY GAME
1 13 DEAD END DRIVE GAME
1 TOMB OF DOOM GAME
1 YAHTZEE GAME
1 WHAT TIME IS IT? GAME
1 FRUSTRATION GAME
1 GO FOR BROKE GAME
1 JUNGLE BUNGLE GAME
1 PAYDAY GAME
1 MYSTERIES OF PEKING GAME
1 CRAZY CROCODILES GAME
1 OPERATION GAME
1 WAR GAME
1 TEENAGE MUTANT HERO TURTLES JIGSAW PUZZLE
1 1000-PIECE RENOIR JIGSAW PUZZLE
1 1000-PIECE GOLF JIGSAW
1 MAYHEM IN MOVIE LAND JIGSAW PUZZLE
1 OCTOPUS WHIRL GAME
1 SHAKE AND MAKE STORIES GAME
1 50-PIECE OCEAN JIGSAW PUZZLE
1 CATS, DOGS, HOGS GAME
1 BUCKAROO GAME
1 SPIROGRAPH SET
1 GUESS WHO? GAME
1 AIR-FIX CUTTY SHARK GAME
1 SCRABBLE FOR JUNIORS GAME
1 OUTRAGE GAME
1 HORNBY SIGNAL BOX GAME
1 MEMO FRENCH ALPHABET GAME
1 LITTLE WORLD SET
1 PARTY PLAY SET
1 ADVENTURE PLAYGROUND TOY TENT
1 KINDER ZAUBERSPIELE MAGIC TRICK SET
1 ACTION MAN TOY FIGURE
27 SETS OF PLAYING CARDS
1 GERMAN CASTLE GAME
1 PINGU JIGSAW
1 BAG OF ASSORTED BALLOONS
1 ANIMAL DOMINOES GAME
2 PINGU MEMO CARD GAME
1 PICTURE DOMINO GAME
1 METAL CHESSBOARD
1 RACING GAME BOARD
2 GAME BOARDS
1 CHILD'S SUBTRACTION LEARNING TOY
1 LOTTO BOX WITH ASSORTED CARD GAMES
1 RED PLASTIC SNOW GLOBE WITH PHOTO FRAME INSIDE
1 TOY POLICE CAR
2 TOY CARPENTRY SETS
1 PULL-ALONG DUCK
1 BOOK OF NURSERY RHYMES
1 TOOL JIGSAW

1 GREEN PLASTIC TOY TORCH
1 YELLOW PLASTIC TOY TRUCK
1 PLASTIC TOY CAR
1 RED METAL TOY TRUCK WITH CRANE
1 SINGER SEWING MACHINE
1 TOY DOLL WITH PINK HAIR
1 BLUE AND RED PLASTIC TOY BATTLESHIP
1 SPEEDO ORANGE AND BLUE ARMBAND
1 TOY PANDA CLOCK
1 WINNIE THE POOH WASHING-UP BOWL
1 PLASTIC TOY SHIELD
1 GREEN AND BLACK PAIR OF FLIPPERS
1 BOX OF BLACK AND YELLOW LEGO
1 WINNIE THE POOH SHOPPING TROLLEY
1 TOY LOCH NESS MONSTER
1 FLUFFY SOFT TOY COW
1 CHICKEN SHAPED RATTLE
1 MUMRAH THUNDERCAT TOY FIGURE
1 RED AND YELLOW SNAKE SOFT TOY
1 MCDONALD'S SQUIRREL TOY
1 SABRINA'S SECRETS BODY GLITTER SET
1 BOTTLE PINK NAIL VARNISH
1 PLASTIC MILKSHAKE MAKER
2 BOXES OF ASSORTED TOOLS
2 MCDONALD'S TOY FIGURES
1 DOG-SHAPED RATTLE
1 BRONZE LIP GLITTER
1 NATIONWIDE BEAR AND OWL LIGHT REFLECTOR
1 MCDONALD'S SOFT TOY BEAR
1 PIECE OF DOLL'S HOUSE KITCHEN FURNITURE
1 FUNFAX CHICK BOOK
1 FUNFAX PIG BOOKS
1 TIME FOR BED LITTLE TIGER BOOK
1 INCOMPLETE WOODEN FLOWER PRESS
1 TOY HORSE
1 RED PLASTIC TOY FIRE ENGINE
1 GREY PLASTIC TIPPER TRUCK
1 YELLOW PLASTIC CRANE ARM
1 ORANGE PLASTIC TOY SHED
1 TOY FARM SET WITH COW AND TRACTOR
1 ORANGE AND BLACK PAIR OF FLIPPERS
1 PURPLE PLASTIC TOY TRUCK CONTAINER
1 GREEN STEAM TRAIN SHAPED RATTLE
1 RED PLASTIC FRENCH TELEPHONE WITH MISSING HANDSET
1 WOODEN HORSE RACING GAME
3 LUDO BOARD GAMES
2 MINI HOT WHEELS TOY SETS
2 CHESS GAMES
1 CRAYOLA ROLLING PAPER PAD
22 MULTICOLOURED MAGNET PAWNS
1 PLASTIC HAIRY KIWI FRUIT
1 PAIR NIKE SUNGLASSES
1 TOY TOOL SET
1 PAIR BELSON WALKIE-TALKIE
1 CHAD VALLEY EMERGENCY VEHICLE TOY SET
1 BLACK MAKE UP BAG
1 YELLOW PLASTIC ROTARY DRILL
2 YELLOW PLASTIC TOY CONVOY VEHICLES
1 HALFORS METAL BONDER
1 MECCANO TOY SET
1 CHIP N DALE GAME
1 RED G-CLAMP
1 SOFT CATERPILLAR RATTLE
1 SOFT BUTTERFLY RATTLE
1 HAIRY CAMEL SOFT TOY
1 OCTOPUS SOFT TOY
2 KOALA BEAR SOFT TOYS
1 GONZO THE MUPPET SOFT TOY
1 RED CAR SOFT TOY
1 RED BLUE AND YELLOW SOFT TOY RATTLE
1 MINIATURE SLUSH PUPPY TOY MACHINE
1 TREE SHAPED SOFT TOY RATTLE
1 MCDONALD'S TOY MONKEY
1 PRAM RATTLE
1 BROWN AND BLACK PLASTIC RIFLE
1 MINIATURE TOY DRESSING TABLE WITH ONE MISSING DOOR
1 INCOMPLETE GIRLZONE TOY SET
1 CUBE SHAPED JIGSAW PUZZLE
1 MCDONALD'S TWEENIE SOFT TOY
1 BROMLEY BUZZ DESIGN BLUE FRISBEE
1 MAP OF BERN
2 TOY POLES FOR DOLL'S HOUSE
1 NAKED DOLL
1 THUNDERBIRDS TRACEY ISLAND TOY
1 PLASTIC BOARD GAME STAND
1 HANGING SPIDERMAN TOY FIGURE
1 PACKET OF CIRCULAR ORANGE STICKERS
1 RED AND SILVER TIARA HAIRCLIP
1 YELLOW TAMBOURINE
1 HOT WHEELS YELLOW CAR

1 PURPLE HEADBAND EMBROIDERED WITH THE NAME SARA
1 PLASTIC JUMBO JET AIRPLANE
1 THOMAS THE TANK ENGINE CARRY CASE
1 PLASTIC DOME FOR UNSPECIFIED GAME
1 BIRILLO MANIA PLASTIC SKITTLES GAME
1 PACK OF TOTAL ACTION EMERGENCY RESCUE FIGURES
1 PACK FREE WHEEL EMERGENCY PATROL FIGURE
1 TOY PABLO JUNIOR CREATIVE CONSTRUCTION SET
1 TOY HIGH PERFORMANCE LORRY
1 LITTER BUGS GAME
2 RED PLASTIC TOY TRACTORS
2 TOY SUPERCARD TRANSPORTER TRUCKS
1 WOODEN TRAY JIGSAW PUZZLE
1 INCOMPLETE TOP OF THE POPS STATIONERY SET
3 ASSORTED PENCIL CASES
1 POCKET MEGA SKETCHER SKETCHBOOK
1 PLASTIC RED BLUE AND YELLOW RATTLE
1 WOODEN JIGSAW PUZZLE
1 ALPHABET STENCIL
3 PINK PLASTIC PLATES
1 WHITE AND BLACK NY BASEBALL CAP
1 BLACK PLASTIC BOTTLE WITH PINK FLOWER
1 PLASTIC LITTLE MISS NAUGHTY OVERALL
1 FLORAL QUILTED WASH BAG
5 LITTLE MERMAID LIPGLOSSES
1 BLACK LIQUID AIR FRESHENER
1 CHRISTMAS DECORATION
1 FRUSTRATION GAME
1 PLAY MAT WITH CHESS DESIGN
1 YELLOW PLASTIC TOY TRAILER
2 B&Q HAMMERS
3 ASSORTED RING BINDERS
2 ROLLS WHITE PACKING TAPE
1 ROLL OF BLACK GAFFER TAPE
50 PLASTIC ZIPLOCK BAGS
1 ROLL OF GREEN GARDENING WIRE
1 LOOKING FOR ANDREW MCCARTHY BOOK
1 WOMANISE THE TYRANNY OF SLENDERNESS BOOK
1 FLAUNTING EXTRAVAGANT QUEEN BOOK
1 TEMPTATION BY MILLS AND BOON BOOK
1 AUTO BIOPSY BOOK
1 PLAYING AWAY BOOK
1 WIZARD JOKES BOOK
1 A PARROT IN THE PEPPER TREE BOOK
1 PUZZLE BOOK
1 CAT'S CRADLE BOOK
1 BONES AND MURDER BOOK
1 THORNY HOUGH BOOK
1 THE PURVEYOR OF ENCHANTMENT BOOK
1 MAD COWS BOOK
1 BEET QUEEN BOOK
1 THE JONAH BOOK
1 DEFINITIVE IQ TEST FOR CATS BOOK
1 GREAT ANIMAL STORIES BOOK
1 THE SWEETSHOP OWNER BOOK
1 THE STUD BOOK
1 FROST IN MAY BOOK
1 FROM THE PILOT SEAT BOOK
1 HEALING PRAYER BOOK
1 PIERROT'S JOURNEY BOOK
1 TAG ALONG TRAIN BOOK
1 JANET JACKSON'S RHYTHM NATION CD
8 VARIOUS STEEL GIRDERS PAINTED WHITE
7 WOODEN PALLETS PARTIALLY PAINTED
3 ASSORTED WOODEN OFF-CUTS
1 THICK PERSPEX SHEET
80 WOODEN PLANKS PAINTED WHITE
90 PLANKS PAINTED WHITE
1 MDF WOODEN BENCH PAINTED WHITE
5 COLOURED WOODEN PLANKS
2 WOODEN PIECES PAINTED WHITE
1 BLUE METAL GAS CANISTER
1 WOODEN DOORSTOP
1 WOODEN PICTURE FRAME
1 BROKEN PLASTIC RASPBERRY
1 METAL DOOR HANDLE
1 METAL BLACK BICYCLE LOCK
1 USED ARTIST'S SPATULA
1 MARCITA DRILL BATTERY IN PLASTIC CASE
1 WHITE-AND-YELLOW DISHCLOTH
1 GREEN PLASTIC DIARY
2 GREY PIECES OF STONE
2 PLASTIC BOXES OF BUSINESS CARDS
1 BLACK METAL OFFICE DESK LAMP
1 SMALL CONTAINER OF UPHOLSTERY NAILS
1 WOODEN SANDING BLOCK WITH SANDPAPER
13 ASSORTED EMPTY CIGAR BOXES
1 MACINTOSH COMPUTER MOUSE
10 PAIRS VINYL TRANSPARENT GLOVES
2 BOXES SCHMINKE ARTIST'S SOFT PASTELS

1 WHITE ELECTRIC KETTLE
1 RED PLASTIC MOULDING TEMPLATE
1 KILNER SUGAR JAR
5 ASSORTED METAL CIGAR BOX LIDS
3 9-VOLT BATTERIES
1 BOX OF DENTAL PLASTER
2 ROLLS OF ELECTRICAL TAPE
2 ROLLS OF FISHING WIRE
1 PACK OF OPENED EXTRA CHEWING GUM
1 SPIRAL-BOUND FOLDER
2 PACKS OF HONEST CABBAGE RESTAURANT MATCHES
8 EMPTY PHOTOGRAPHIC PAPER FOLDERS
2 ILFORD PHOTOGRAPHIC PAPER PACKS
3 PLASTIC SLIDE TRAYS
1 TUBE GREEN ACRYLIC PAINT
1 MATEX DRILL BIT SHARPENER
1 KURE COLOUR PERMANENT MARKER PEN
1 RED PLASTIC TIN OF PAINT
1 GLUE GUN STICK
1 ROLL OF WHITE DOUBLE-SIDED TAPE
1 ROLL OF MASKING TAPE
1 ROLL OF BROWN TAPE
1 BOTTLE OF GREY FLANNEL EAU DE TOILETTE
1 PLASTIC BOTTLE OF ACRYLIC BLUE PAINT
1 PLASTIC BOTTLE OF ACRYLIC GREEN PAINT
1 HOMEDECK METALLIC KEYBOARD
1 TIN OF VINYL MATT PAINT
1 ROLL OF BLACK CELLO-TAPE
1 LIVING MUSIC MAGAZINE SPRING 2000
1 TEXT PANEL: TOMOKO TAKAHASHI, LEARNING HOW TO DRIVE
1 PERSPEX SIGN
1 CAPITAL LIFE NEWSPAPER FEBRUARY 23, 2001
1 TIN OF BRILLIANT WHITE EGGSHELL PAINT
1 SYSTEM 3 ACRYLIC COPPER PAINT IN PLASTIC BOTTLE
1 LUCASCRYL ACRYLIC WHITE PAINT
10 EMPTY SAINSBURYS PASTA SAUCE CONTAINERS
1 CLEAR PLASTIC MEASURING BUCKET
1 WHITE PLASTIC BUCKET
1 FLASK OF GALLERIA ACRYLIC RED COLOUR
1 MELTED PLASTIC CAR LIGHT
1 HOT WHEELS CAR
1 PINK, BLUE AND GREEN PLASTIC TOILETRY BAG
1 RUSTY METAL MUDGUARD FROM CHILD'S BICYCLE
2 PLASTIC PARTS OF GREY TOY TRACK
1 STONE ASHTRAY
1 EMPTY PLASTIC NAYA SPRING WATER BOTTLE
1 EMPTY PAPER COFFEE CUP
1 PART FROM TRAVEL CONNECT FOUR GAME
1 SILVER PLASTIC TOY FENCE
1 GREY PLASTIC TOY TOOL CASE
1 UNITED AIRLINES FREIGHT TOYS
1 BROWN PLASTIC MINIATURE TELESCOPE
1 RED PLASTIC DOLL'S STILETTO SHOE
1 GREEN PLASTIC PUZZLE
1 WHITE LIGHTER
1 BRASS CANDLEHOLDER
1 PERMANENT BLUE MARKER PEN
1 SEEN IT ALL SERVICES LTD LEAFLET
1 VINAKAL VINYL PAINTING CHART
2 PLASTIC BOLTS
1 BLACK PLASTIC MINIATURE COAL TRAIN TOY
1 BROWN PLASTIC TOY PLANK
1 SYTEMBOLAGET SWEDISH CALENDAR SHEET, MARCH 2001
1 ITALIAN FESTIVAL 1999 LEAFLET
1 WORKAID VOLUNTARY SERVICES LEAFLET
1 INSTRUCTION SHEET FOR BARBIE BIKE
1 PLASTIC BALL SHAPED SPRAY BOTTLE
2 WOODEN STOOLS
1 RUSTY RED CAR JACK
1 SPARE TRUCK TYRE
25 CHILDREN'S WOODEN CHAIRS
1 COMPUTER MONITOR
1 COMPUTER MOUSE
1 COMPUTER KEYBOARD
1 OXYGEN BOTTLE ON RUSTY METALLIC STAND
1 THOMSON-PREFERRED AGENT BROKEN GLASS SIGN
1 EPSON COMPUTER PRINTER
2 EMPTY BLACK PLASTIC TOOL TRAYS
1 GREY PLASTIC CONTAINER
1 ROLL OF NON-BLEACHED THIN CARDBOARD
7 EMPTY ASSORTED GLASS JAM JARS
1 SAINSBURY'S RED THAI SOUP EMPTY CONTAINER
1 ROLL OF WHITE AND RED FRAGILE TAPE
2 PLASTIC SPRAY CANS LIDS
1 RED PLASTIC BOX
1 MITSUBISHI PC MOTHERBOARD
1 WOODEN TABLE
1 HITACHI TV
2 CHILDREN'S METAL TABLES
2 RED PLASTIC WOVEN CONTAINERS

1 PLASTIC CONTAINER WITH BROKEN HANDLE
1 DIPLOMAT DISHWASHER
2 AQUARIUS 1100 WASHING MACHINES
1 CREDA COOKER
1 BEKO FRIDGE
1 CARDBOARD SIGN
1 WORTHINGTON REFRIGERATOR
1 LOW WOODEN TABLE
1 PIECE OF CARDBOARD WITH HANDWRITTEN MARKINGS
1 ROUND CHILD'S TABLE
1 BROKEN CHRISTMAS TREE DECORATION
1 PLASTIC WASHING MACHINE LID
1 GLASS WASHING MACHINE LID
2 BLUE METAL BOLTS
1 MATSUI MICROWAVE
1 TANDBERG REEL-TO-REEL TAPE RECORDER
1 BROWN SOFT TOY STUFFED CAMEL
1 STUFFED SOFT TOY KOALA
1 BLACK PLASTIC TOY HORSE
1 RED PLASTIC TOY BOWLING BALL
1 WASHING MACHINE MOTOR
1 UNIDENTIFIED PIECE OF METAL
1 BROWN METAL MUSIC STAND WITH WHEELS
1 SOFT TOY INSECT WITH BELLS
1 WOODEN CHILD'S COAT HANGER
1 MOSCOW BOOK
1 ORIENTAL GARDENS BOOK
1 SUGAR ROSES FOR CAKES BOOK
1 TRANSPORT BOOK
1 BOOK NEUWE ENCYCLOPAEDIA VAN DER BIJBEL
1 WORK INDUSTRY SCHOOL BOOK
1 MEIN FRAGEBUCH VON GOTT BOOK
1 MEIN FRAGEBUCH VON DER BIBEL BOOK
2 THE ESSENTIAL BOOK OF WOODWORK BOOKS
1 BROTHERS AND SISTERS BOOK
1 INISHOWEN BOOK
1 SPACE: NOW AND INTO THE FUTURE SCHOOL BOOK
1 EL LIBRO COMPLETO DEL TARO BOOK
1 WAS SEIGT MIR DEIN GESICHT?BOOK
1 AIRPLANES SCHOOL BOOK
3 SKYSCRAPERS SCHOOL BOOKS
1 CONTAINER GARDEN BOOK
1 THE TEMPLE BOOK
1 SPORT AND LEISURE SCHOOL BOOK
1 TRANSPORTATION: NOW AND INTO THE FUTURE SCHOOL BOOK
1 O MISERIO DE MILTON BOOK
1 PLANTS FOR THE DRY GARDEN BOOK
1 MEDICINE: NOW AND INTO THE FUTURE SCHOOL BOOK
1 THE CONTROLS SCHOOL BOOK
2 SPEEDY MACHINES BOATS BOOK
1 LANDSLIDES AND AVALANCHES SCHOOL BOOK
1 HET RUIMTE VEER BOOK
1 ZDOBYC FACETA BOOK
1 AIRCRAFT SCHOOL BOOK
1 THE OUTER SHELL SCHOOL BOOK
1 LIVSGLAEDE BOOK
1 FREIHET BOOK
1 DONEGAL ISLANDS BOOK
1 WITH LOVE TO DAD BOOK
1 GREEN AND BLACK PLASTIC TRAY
1 OLD AWL
1 ORANGE CINDY DOLL CARAVAN WITH ONE SIDE MISSING
2 CAR TYRES
1 CERAMIC SINK
1 HOLDER FOR FLUORESCENT BULB
1 UNIDENTIFIED CAR PART
1 CLUTCH AND BREAK PEDAL
1 METAL CHIMNEY BREAST
1 WOODEN DOLL'S HOUSE
1 FOLDABLE BED
1 GLASS CUPBOARD DOOR
1 METAL DUSTBIN LID
3 CAR RIMS
1 RUSTY METAL LAWNMOWER
3 DRIVE SHAFT CAR PARTS
1 METAL SHEET
1 BAG OF BOTTLES
2 METAL BINS
2 PLASTIC VACUUM PARTS
1 BOX OF UNIDENTIFIED RUSTY METAL
1 UNIDENTIFIED PLASTIC ITEM
1 SMALL WOODEN RAMP
1 PLASTIC DISPENSING MACHINE
1 RADIATOR
1 WHITE ROLLER BLIND
2 PIECES OF COPPER PIPING WITH TAPS ATTACHED
1 GEARBOX
3 METAL WHEELS
1 FOLDAWAY METAL CHAIR
1 WOODEN WINDOW FRAME

1 PLASTIC KETTLE
1 METAL CAR PART
1 METAL MOP BUCKET
1 METAL DUSTBIN LID
2 CABLE ROLLERS
1 METAL DRUM
1 GREY METAL CABINET
1 VENETIAN BLINDS
1 GEARBOX WITH DRIVE SHAFT
1 PLASTIC AND METAL UNIDENTIFIED CAR PART
1 ROLL OF RUBBER SHEETING
1 BROWN PLASTIC TRAY
1 VOLTAGE SELECTION UNIT
1 BROWN VACUUM CLEANER
1 BLACK ANGLEPOISE LAMP
1 WHITE PLASTIC WATER CONTAINER
1 SMALL YELLOW CAR-SHAPED TOY
1 WHITE LAMP STAND
1 BABY BATH
1 SODA STREAM MACHINE
1 COMPUTER HARD DRIVE
1 BLACK METAL ROOF RACK
1 EPSON PRINTER
2 PIECES OF BLUE TUBING
1 BROWN PLASTIC FILING TRAY
1 METAL TABLE
1 PANASONIC VCR
2 POLYSTYRENE COLUMNS
1 CHILD'S UPHOLSTERED CHAIR
1 METAL GRILL APPROX 1 X 1M
1 BAG OF UNIDENTIFIABLE MATERIAL
1 SHEET OF ALUMINIUM APPROX 1 X 1M
1 WIRE MESH FENCE PART
1 KITCHEN SPONGE
1 CARDBOARD TEMPLATE WITH MUSICAL NOTES
1 ROLLER BLIND
1 WOODEN BROOM
1 CARDBOARD SHEET
APPROXIMATELY 200 A2 SHEETS WITH PRINT OF HOUSE
4 GREY FOLDING OFFICE BOXES
2 ASSORTED BROWN PAPER SHEETS
1 CARDBOARD CUT-OUT IN SHAPE OF A VASE
2 SHEETS OF CARDBOARD
1 REAM A2 PINK PAPER
1 REAM A2 YELLOW PAPER
1 CHRISTMAS CARD FROM PRINTERS ON A3 SHEET
APPROXIMATELY 20 SHEETS OF A4 WHITE PAPER
1 REAM OF A2 BLUE PAPER
1 REAM OF A2 TAUPE PAPER
1 REAM OF A3 YELLOW PAPER
A2 DARK BLUE PAPER
A2 LIGHT PINK PAPER
1 PAIR OF METAL SHEEP SHEARS
1 PAIR OF GREEN WELLINGTON BOOTS
1 TOY CHAINSAW
2 BAGS OF ASSORTED KITCHEN SPONGES AND PAPER CUPS
1 DREAM CITY PLASTIC TOY CITY WITH FIGURES AND VEHICLES
3 GIANT CRANE TOY CRANES
1 TESCO PLASTIC WASHING MACHINE
1 TESCO PLASTIC OVEN
1 ASTROLOGY BOARD GAME
1 TONGUE TANGO BOARD GAME
1 EASY MONEY BOARD GAME
1 DING BATS BOARD GAME
APPROXIMATELY 50 ASSORTED TOY TRUCKS
1 LARGE LORRY TOY
1 FARM PLAY SET TOY
1 BABY DRIVER GAME
2 BATTLES AND COMMANDS GAME
1 FARM PLAYER GAME
1 COMMAND FIELD TENT
1 TURBO RACING SPORTS CAR SET
1 PLAY FOOD BUCKET
1 SET OF MEGA BLOCKS
1 PLASTIC SUPERMARKET TROLLEY WITH ASSORTED PLASTIC FOOD
10 PLASTIC COINS
1 BLUE TRAY WITH RED HANDLES
1 SEA BATTLE BOARD GAME
1 YELLOW PLASTIC TRAILER
1 PLASTIC TOY TILL
1 PIECE OF CHICKEN WIRE
1 TV
1 YELLOW PLASTIC JCB
1 TIPPER TRUCK
1 PLASTIC WRAPPING FILM WITH WHITE FLOWER PRINT
1 METAL TIPPER TRUCK TOY
1 PLASTIC CEMENT MIXER TOY
2 MINIATURE WOODEN ROCKING CHAIRS
1 TOY CONSTRUCTION BUILDING SITE SET
1 TESCO MUSICAL TEA SET

1 MONOPOLY GAME
1 GO FOR BROKE GAME
1 GAME OF LIFE BOARD GAME
6 PACKS OF PHOTOGRAPHS
1 ROLL OF FILM
1 CARRIER BAG FULL OF ASSORTED CHRISTMAS DECORATIONS
1 BAG OF BLACK CIRCULAR RUBBER DISKS
1 PORTABLE HEATER
1 ROLL OF RUBBER CABLE
1 PANASONIC VCR
1 PLASTIC RACK FOR PLATES
1 PINK PLASTIC WASTEBASKET
1 SMALL BROWN CERAMIC URN
1 CLEAR GLASS FLAGON
1 WINDSCREEN WIPER
1 BLACK PLASTIC STEERING WHEEL
1 DIPSTICK
1 WHITE PLASTIC WATER TANK FOR CAR
1 UNIDENTIFIED CAR PART WITH ATTACHED WATER TANK
10 UNIDENTIFIED CAR PARTS
1 SUPER SHOP MODERN TOY KITCHEN
2 PLASTIC MINIATURE FIGURES
1 BLACK PLASTIC HANGER
1 BOXED TOY
1 BOXED GAME OF CHESS V
1 FAKE CHRISTMAS TREE
1 MACHINE FOR FOLDING METAL
1 NEC TV
1 PIECE OF MDF
1 BROKEN WOODEN SHELF UNIT
1 IMITATION SILVER CHARM
1 GOLDEN CLIP-ON EARRING
1 LIGHT BLUE CERAMIC SAUCER
1 BROKEN IMITATION SILVER RING
1 CERAMIC HEN
1 OFF-WHITE VEST WITH BROWN AND YELLOW RIBBONS
1 CARRIER BAG OF ASSORTED FAKE FLOWERS
1 SMALL IMITATION SILVER BRACELET
1 PAIR OF IMITATION PEARL EARRINGS
1 PAIR OF YELLOW PLASTIC EARRINGS
1 IMITATION SILVER BRACELET WITH PINK STONES
1 PAIR OF METAL FLOWER EARRINGS
1 PAIR OF PLASTIC SEASHELL EARRINGS
1 PART OF NECKLACE
2 PLASTIC CUFFLINKS
1 SILVER NECKLACE CHAIN
1 DR MARTENS SHOE INSERT
6 ASSORTED METALLIC AND PLASTIC CHARMS
1 GLASS CROSS
1 IMITATION SILVER EARRING
1 EARRING
1 EMPTY CAMERA CASE
1 CERAMIC CHARM
1 NOKIA MOBILE PHONE COVER
1 EMPTY RING BOX
1 ROLL OF SILVER TAPE
1 PLASTIC TRAY
1 CHILD'S BOOK
1 PLASTIC EARRING
1 MIRROR WITH WOODEN FRAME
1 BOOK
1 BOOK OF POEMS
2 HANDLES FOR BAG
1 RED SILK TIE
1 RED BRACELET
1 BROWN METAL CIGARETTE CASE
1 DOLL'S PILLOW
2 PLATES WITH FLOWER PATTERN
1 CHINA ASHTRAY
1 STATUE OF GOLFING FIGURE
1 BRONZE-COLOURED BUST
1 GOLD-COLOURED BROOCH
1 RED PLASTIC CARRYING CASE
2 RED LEATHER FOLDER
2 VOLKSWAGEN HUBCAPS
2 UNIDENTIFIED CAR PARTS
1 RED FIRE EXTINGUISHER HOUSING
1 NEW TESTAMENT BIBLE
1 BROWN GLASS FLAGON
1 BOOK OF LOVE STORIES
1 THE READINGS WITH JULIAN OF NORWICH BOOK
2 SWAHILI DICTIONARIES
1 LATHOM PARK CHAPEL LEAFLET
1 LEEDS AND LIVERPOOL CANAL LEAFLET
1 LIVERPOOL CATHEDRAL LEAFLET
1 LIGHT BROWN LEATHER FILE CASE
1 ORANGE WOODEN FLOWER
1 CERAMIC FLASK WITH STRING ATTACHED
1 CERAMIC PLATE WITH RED, WHITE AND BLUE BIRD IMAGE
1 WOODEN BROOM

ASSORTED WHITE TELEPHONE CABLE
1 BEIGE OFFICE TELEPHONE
1 BLACK ADAPTOR
3 TELEPHONE EXTENSIONS
1 SET OF INSTRUCTIONS FOR FARALLON
1 SET OF INSTRUCTIONS FOR CONSORT 1+4
1 BROWN ENVELOPE
1 RED AND WHITE PLASTIC BIKE LIGHT
1 BLACK BOW TIE
1 TEXTILE BADGE
1 OVAL HAND MIRROR
2 LAVENDER BAGS
5 BADMINTON RACKETS
4 TENNIS RACKETS
1 CANDLEHOLDER
1 ROUND METAL DISH
1 EMPTY PLASTIC CASSETTE BOX
2 POLYSTYRENE BICYCLE HELMETS
2 SMALL FLUORESCENT LIGHTS
1 ROLL OF WHITE ELECTRICAL TAPE
2 DIRTY PAINTBRUSHES
1 PLASTIC WALL PLAQUE
1 RED WATERING CAN SHAPED LIKE ROOF OF HOUSE
1 TOY STEERING WHEEL
1 PACK OF MINIATURE FOOD ON PLATE TOY
1 KEY RING
1 PLASTIC FIGURE
1 PLASTIC BAKER FIGURE
1 UNIDENTIFIED PART OF CHILD'S TOY
1 DOLL CARRYING GREEN AND WHITE SKIPPING ROPE
1 SMALL BROWN FUR MONKEY
1 WHITE PLASTIC CHIPMUNK
1 SMALL RED PLASTIC TOWER
1 PLASTIC SPANISH FIGURE
1 PLASTIC ASTRONAUT FIGURE
1 GREY MECHANICAL MOUSE
1 SQUIRREL GLOVE PUPPET
2 ACTION FIGURES
1 CHILD'S WHEELBARROW
1 TRAVEL CLUEDO GAME
APPROXIMATELY 100 TWEEZERS
1 EMPTY HONGHE BRAND CIGARETTE PACKET
1 EMPTY FUJI FILM PACK
1 MINI CD CASE
1 PIECE OF DRIFTWOOD
1 STRAW HAT FOR A DOLL
4 ASSORTED CHESS PIECES
1 LIGHT BULB HOLDER SHAPED LIKE BLACKBERRY
1 SMALL GREY-AND-WHITE RUBBER SHARK
1 PLASTIC LID
1 UNIDENTIFIED YELLOW AND BLACK PLASTIC ITEM
1 BROWN PAPER BAG WITH BARBIE LOGO
1 SAUCEPAN
1 PLASTIC DOG
1 PART OF TOY TRUCK
1 RED CLOTH WITH CHINON LOGO
1 PACK OF RED, WHITE AND GREEN COCKTAIL STICKS
1 MINIATURE DUSTBIN LID
2 PLASTIC COINS
1 WOODEN BLUE FIGURE
2 COLOURED PLASTIC DISKS
1 SMALL WHITE DESK LAMP
1 MY TREASURE HUNT GAME
1 LARGE ALUMINIUM FRYING PAN

Tomoko Takahashi and the Serpentine Gallery would like to thank the following for contributing materials to this project:

Hales Gallery
The Royal Parks, in particular Nick Butler
Victoria & Albert Museum, London, and Martin Barnes
Workaid, Amersham, particularly Ray Richards and Silvia Parrot
Ozone Friends, Barking, especially Ray Barwick
Toyhouse Libraries Association of Tower Hamlets, and Pip Pinhorn
Barnardo's, South Woodford, and Tracy Purcell
1,000,000 mph, London, in particular Dallas Seitz
Hammersmith and Fulham MIND, Repaint scheme, and Rosanna Casorerio
Chris Caris Enterprises, London, and Christine Carey
Queensbridge School, Hackney
Sebright School, Hackney
Merry-Go-Round, Hackney
Children's Warehouse and Art Store, Newcastle
Fordham Gallery, London
Car-boot sales at Holloway, Wimbledon Greyhound Stadium, New Covent
        Garden Market, St Augustine's School in Kilburn, and Chestnut
        School and Alwyn School in Bermondsey
Clem Price-Thomas
Colin Saggers
Martyn Silver
Malcolm J Brodie
David McCracken
Neil Astley
Julia Barton
Nick Vidovic
Barbara Patkova
Christine MacGregor
And skips in and around London for yielding untold treasures

Biography

Born Tokyo, 1966
BA Fine Art, Goldsmiths College, London, 1991–94
Higher Diploma, Postgraduate Study in Sculpture, Slade School of Fine Art, London, 1994–96
Lives and works in London

Selected solo exhibitions

1997
Company Deal, Claydon Heeley International, London
Untitled, Beaconsfield, London
1998
Info Only, Tablet, London
Clockwork at Hales, Hales Gallery, London
The Drawing Room, The Drawing Center, New York
Staff Stuff, Staff USA, New York
1999
Dark Room at Stills (for Clifford Haynes), Stills Gallery, Edinburgh
Office Work (organized by Roomade), Century Centre, Antwerp, Belgium
Site Work, Galeria Pedro Cera, Lisbon
In.Form, Lift Gallery, London
Grant Selwyn Fine Art, Los Angeles
Entwistle Gallery, London
The Day of Patience (with Ella Gibbs), belt a space in between, London
2000
Word Perhect (with Jon Pollard), commissioned by Chisenhale Gallery, London and e-2, London
2001
Galleri Charlotte Lund, Stockholm
2002
Deep Sea Diving, Kunsthalle Bern, Switzerland
Auditorium Piece, UCLA Hammer Museum, Los Angeles

Selected group exhibitions

1995
Shave '95, Shave Farm, Somerset, England
Memory '95, Riverside Studios, London
1997
EAST International, Norwich Gallery, England
Low Maintenance & High Precision, Hales Gallery, London
Gonzo, Old Bethnal Green Police Station, London
1998
The Campaign Against Living Miserably, Royal College of Art, London
View (Four), Mary Boone Gallery, New York
The Best Surprise is No Surprise (organized by Mayday Productions), Holiday Inn China Town, New York
1999
Neurotic Realism, Saatchi Gallery, London
Laboratorium, Antwerp, Belgium
Generation Z, PS1, New York
48 Hours (with Ella Gibbs), Tablet, London

2000

Found Wanting, Atlanta Contemporary Art Center, Georgia
Artworkers, Oriel Mostyn Gallery and Newlyn Art Gallery, Llandudno, Wales
Beautiful, Oxo Tower Wharf, London
Parklight, Clissold Park, London
Turner Prize, Tate Britain, London

2002

Ideal Home, Gimpel Fils, London
A Record of Events, Hales Gallery, London
Room for Improvement, Craft Museum, New Delhi
International Artists Fellowship Exhibition, Upriver Loft, Kunming, China and Gasworks, London
Sprawl, The Contemporary Arts Center, Cincinnati, Ohio

2003

Living Inside the Grid, New Museum of Contemporary Art, New York
Charlie's Place, Annely Juda Fine Art, London

2004

Ticker Tape Parade Without Parade 2 (with Rupert Carey), Roppongi Crossing, Mori Art Museum, Tokyo
No Money, Kunsthalle zu Kiel, Germany

Bibliography

Selected books and catalogues

1999

New Neurotic Realism. Essay by Dick Price. London: Saatchi Gallery
High Art Lite. Julian Stallabrass. London: Verso

2000

Turner Prize 2000. Essays by Mary Horlock, Jemima Montagu and Ben Tufnell. London: Tate
Artworkers. Essay by Melissa Feldman. Llandudno: Oriel Mostyn Gallery

2002

The Catalogue of Allmost All the Works Done By… Tomoko Takahashi (Between 1985–2002). Essays by Bernhard Fibicher and David Lillington. Bern: Kunsthalle Bern
29.01.02–10.03.02. Interviews by Robert Loder and Ye Yong Qing. London: Triangle Arts Trust

2004

No Money. Dirk Luckow, ed. Kiel: Kunsthalle zu Kiel

Selected artist's books

1999

The Booklet of Patience. Ella Gibbs and Tomoko Takahashi. London: Tablet
The Booklet of Patience. Ella Gibbs and Tomoko Takahashi. London: belt a space in between

2000

The Booklet of Patience. Ella Gibbs and Tomoko Takahashi. London: Tate
The One and Only Users' Guide for Word Perhect. Tomoko Takahashi. London: e-2 and Chisenhale Gallery
Handbook of Turun Taidemuseo Abo Konstmuseum Turku Art Museum. Tomoko Takahashi, ed. London: Beaconsfield

Selected articles and reviews

1997
'Company Deal'. *The Times*, April 19
'Company Deal'. *Shukan Shincho*, May 22
'This Work of Art Won £5000 First Prize'. *Eastern Daily Press*, July 18
'EAST'. *The Times*, July 19
'EAST'. *Daily Mail*, July 19
'EAST'. *Daily Telegraph*, July 19
'EAST'. *The Times*, July 30
'Low Maintenance'. *Time Out*, August 7
David Burrows. 'Low Maintenance & High Precision'. *Art Monthly*, September, pp 39–40
Mark Currah. 'Tomoko Takahashi'. *Time Out*, November 14

1998
Louisa Buck. 'Faces to Watch in 1998'. *New Statesman*, January 2, p 24
Maite Lores. 'Other Voices, Other Places'. *Contemporary Visual Arts*, issue 17, pp 45–49
Julian Stallabrass. 'Tomoko Takahashi'. *Artist's Newsletter*, February, p 17
Maite Lores. 'Tomoko Takahashi: A Project for the New Tabernacle'. *Contemporary Visual Arts*, Issue 19, p 79
Rachel Withers. 'Tomoko Takahashi'. *Frieze*, March–April, p 84
Louisa Buck. 'Tomoko Takahashi'. *Artforum*, Summer, pp 120–21
David Humphrey. 'New York Fax'. *Art Issues*, no 54, September–October, pp 32–33
Franklin Sirmans. 'Tomoko Takahashi: The Drawing Center's Drawing Room'. *Flash Art*, October, p 124
Jerry Saltz. 'Tomoko Takahashi: Staff Stuff'. *Time Out New York*, November 10

1999
'Boys' Zone'. *Time Out*, January 13
Kate Mikhail. 'Rubbish, Absolute Rubbish'. *The Independent*, January 5
Richard Cork. 'Last Orders in the Wasteland'. *The Times*, January 12
Max Andrews. 'Die Young Stay Pretty and Neurotic Realism Part 1'. *Contemporary Visual Arts*, Issue 22, pp 60–61
Jo Manby. 'Dossier of a Madwoman'. *Make: The Magazine of Women's Art*, June–August, pp 12–14
'Lift/Entwistle'. *Time Out*, August 18
Martin Herbert. 'Chaos Theory'. *Contemporary Visual Arts*, Issue 26, pp 22–27
James Hall. 'Neurotic Realism Part I'. *Artforum*, October, pp 155–56
Robert Preece. 'Tomoko Takahashi: In the Eye of the Tornado'. *Sculpture*, November, pp 10–11

2000
Louisa Buck. 'And They Don't Use Dead Animals'. *Observer Magazine*, March 19
Robert Preece. 'Staging Controlled Chaos'. *Art Asia Pacific*, Issue 25, pp 51–55
Claire Bishop. 'Tomoko Takahashi, Accumulation of Memories'. *Flash Art*, March–April, pp 94–95
Michael Gibbs. 'I Can't Find It'. *Art Monthly*, July–August, p 60
Stephen Bury. 'e Books'. *Art Monthly*, November, pp 42–43
Claire Bishop. 'Tomoko Takahashi'. *Art Text*, December 2000–January 2001, p 80

2001
Gemma de Cruz. 'The Artists' Champion'. *Art Review*, April, pp 32–35
Lisa Panting. 'Tomoko Takahashi'. *Art Monthly*, May, pp 36–37

2003
Meghan Dailey. 'Living Inside the Grid'. *Artforum*, May, pp 171–72
Merrily Kerr. 'Living Inside the Grid'. *Flash Art*, May–June, p 88

2004
Colette Chattopadhyay. 'Tomoko Takahashi'. *Sculpture*, January–February, p 73

Rosina Lee Yue and Bert A Lies, Jr
Poju and Anita Zabludowicz

Benefactors

Heinz and Simone Ackermans
Shane Akeroyd
Max Alexander and Anna Bateson
Alan and Charlotte Artus
Azia Chatila
James M Bartos
Anne Best
Roger and Beverley Bevan
Lavinia Calza Beveridge
David and Janice Blackburn
Anthony and Gisela Bloom
John and Jean Botts
Marcus Boyle
Vanessa Branson
Robert Bransten
Mrs Conchita Broomfield
Benjamin Brown
Mr and Mrs Charles Brown
Ossi and Paul Burger
John and Susan Burns
Marlene Burston
Mr and Mrs Philip Byrne
Jonathon P Carroll
Andrew Cecil
Monkey Chambers
Mr and Mrs Giuseppe Ciardi
Dr and Mrs David Cohen
Sadie Coles
Louise-Anne Comeau
Carole and Neville Conrad
Sulina and Matthew Conrad
Simon Copsey
Alexander Corcoran
Pilar Corrias and Adam Prideaux
Gul Coskun
Loraine da Costa
Thomas Croft
Mr and Mrs Cuniberti
Joan Curci
Linda and Ronald F Daitz
Helen and Colin David
Ellynne Dec and Andrea Prat
Neil Duckworth
Denise Dumas
Adrienne Dumas
Lance Entwistle
Mike Fairbrass
Mr and Mrs Mark Fenwick
Harry and Ruth Fitzgibbons
Ruth Finch
David and Jane Fletcher
Bruce and Janet Flohr
Robert Forrest
Joscelyn and Edwin Fox
Eric and Louise Franck
Honor Fraser

James Freedman and Anna Kissin
Albert and Lyn Fuss
David Gill
Barbara Gladstone
Glovers Solicitors
Mr and Mrs John Gordon
Dimitri J Goulandris
Francesco Grana and Simona Fantinelli
Mrs Marcia Green
Richard and Linda Grosse
The Bryan Guinness Charitable Trust
Philip Gumuchdjian
Sascha Hackel and Marcus Bury
Abel G Halpern and Helen Chung-Halpern
Louise Hallett
Mr and Mrs Rupert Hambro
Mr and Mrs Antony Harbour
Susan Harris
Mr and Mrs Rick Hayward
Thomas Healy and Fred Hochberg
Marianne Holtermann
Mrs Martha Hummer-Bradley
Montague Hurst Charitable Trust
Mr Michael and Lady Miranda Hutchinson
Iraj and Eva Ispahani
Nicola Jacobs and Tony Schlesinger
Mrs Christine Johnston
Susie Jubb
John Kaldor and Naomi Milgrom
Howard and Linda Karshan
James and Clare Kirkman
Tim and Dominique Kirkman
Mr and Mrs Charles Kirwan-Taylor
Mickey and Jeanne Klein
Herbert and Sybil Kretzmer
The Landau Foundation
Britt Lintner
Barbara Lloyd and Judy Collins
Peder Lund
Steve and Fran Magee
Claude Mandel and Maggie Mechlinski
Mr Otto Julius Maier and Mrs Michèle
    Claudel-Maier
The Lord and Lady Marks
Mr and Mrs Stephen Mather
James and Viviane Mayor
Warren and Victoria Miro
Susan and Claus Moehlmann
Jen Moores
Crissij van den Munckhof
Richard Nagy and Caroline Schmidt
Andrei Navrozov
Marian and Hugh Nineham
Georgia Oetker
Tamiko Onozawa
Mr and Mrs Nicholas Oppenheim
Linda Pace
Desmond Page and Asun Gelardin
Maureen Paley
Dominic Palfreyman

Midge and Simon Palley
Kathrine Palmer
William Palmer
Andrew and Jane Partridge
Julia Peyton-Jones
George and Carolyn Pincus
Ben and Georgie Pincus
Nyda and Oliver Prenn
Sophie Price
Mathew and Angela Prichard
Max Reed
Michael Rich
John and Jill Ritblat
Jacqueline and Nicholas Roe
Victoria, Lady de Rothschild
James Roundell and Bona Montagu
Rolf and Maryam Sachs
Nigel and Annette Sacks
Michael and Julia Samuel
Isabelle Schiavi
Joana and Henrik Schliemann
Glenn Scott Wright
Martin and Elise Smith
Sotheby's
Mr and Mrs Jean-Marc Spitalier
Bina and Philippe von Stauffenberg
Simone and Robert Suss
Emma Tennant and Tim Owens
The Thames Wharf Charity
Christian and Sarah von Thun-Hohenstein
Britt Tidelius
Suzanne Togna
Melissa Ulfane
Ashley and Lisa Unwin
David and Emma Verey
Mr and Mrs Ludovic de Walden
Audrey Wallrock
Pierre and Ziba de Weck
Lord and Lady John Wellesley
Alannah Weston
Helen Ytuarte White
Charles and Kathryn Wickham
Robin Wight and Anastasia Alexander
Martha and David Winfield
Richard and Astrid Wolman
Chad Wollen and Sian Davies
Nabil N Zaouk
Andrzej and Jill Zarzycki

And Patrons and Benefactors
who wish to remain anonymous

This catalogue is published to accompany
Tomoko Takahashi **at the Serpentine Gallery**
22 February – 10 April 2005

Curated by Rochelle Steiner, Chief Curator
Organized by Kathryn Rattee, Exhibition Organizer
Julia Peyton-Jones, Director

Catalogue designed by KerrlNoble, London
Printed in Great Britain by FS Moore Limited
Prepared and published by the Serpentine Gallery, London

Serpentine Gallery

Kensington Gardens
London W2 3XA
T +44 (0)20 7402 6075
F +44 (0)20 7402 4103
www.serpentinegallery.org

ISBN 1-905190-02-6

Supported by

With additional generous support from
Mr and Mrs Federico Ceretti
Guy and Marion Naggar
The Speyer Family Foundation, Inc

The Serpentine Gallery is funded by